ECUMENICAL MARRIAGE & REMARRIAGE

ECUMENICAL
Marriage
&
Remarriage

Gifts and Challenges to the Churches

MICHAEL LAWLER

XXIII

TWENTY-THIRD PUBLICATIONS

Mystic, Connecticut

Twenty-Third Publications
185 Willow Street
P.O. Box 180
Mystic, CT 06355
(203) 536-2611

ISBN 0-89622-441-4
Library of Congress Catalog Card No 90-70353

PREFACE

I have a group of friends with whom I regularly converse, Charles and Maureen, Bill and Gail, and Peter and Anne (the names have been changed to protect the less than innocent). Charles and Maureen are cradle Catholics; Bill is a convert to Catholicism and Gail is a staunch Presbyterian; Peter is a Lutheran and Anne a charismatic Catholic. Charles and Maureen are happily married in what they smugly call a Catholic marriage, a marriage in which both spouses are "baptized Catholics" (their term). Bill and Gail are equally happily married in what all four have learned, and are content, to call a "mixed marriage" but which I am trying to teach them to call and to accept as an "ecumenical" marriage. Peter and Anne are both in their second marriage, their former spouses still being very much alive.

Our respective marital situations (I also am happily married) make marriage, both Catholic and ecumenical, a frequent subject of conversation and debate. When that debate is about the theological (frequently misnamed "religious") differences between Presbyterian Gail and the rest of us, it can become quite heated. It also can become quite unproductive, for the "theological" information the debaters bring with them is no more than broad confessional generalizations, more appropriately named "prejudices."

Succumbing to Gail's unrelenting pressure, I recently agreed to give a theological address on Christian marriage to an ecumenical gathering. At about the same time, I began to direct a study of Christian marriage with two students planning to marry, one a Catholic, the other a Baptist. It was not long before they reported, with typical undergraduate acerbity, the results of their "research." They found many church pamphlets with lots of dos and don'ts, but little in the way of positive theological and pastoral instruction. I carried that young, Christian observation with me to my ecumenical presentation.

My feeling then, and now, is well summed by Rev. George Kilcourse in his presentation to the 1988 International Conference of Associations of Interchurch Families: "It would not be an exaggeration to describe the dilemma of interchurch couples and families in the past two decades in the U.S. as the product of incomparable pastoral malpractice. Virtually no post-ceremonial pastoral care has been addressed or provided for them."[1]

It is in response to this pastoral "malpractice" that I offer this book.

I intend this work to be both theological and pastoral. I offer it in the hope that it will provide some theologically-based, pastoral self-help to those many Christians who are either contemplating or already living an ecumenical marriage, or have entered into a second marriage. I offer it in the hope that the churches will forego merely bureaucratic cooperation and move to authentic interchurch commitment on these issues. Finally, I offer it in the hope that all Christians and their churches will come to realize clearly and to feel deeply that the true dilemma they face is not mixed marriage or remarriage but the divisions that exist among Christians. The core problem is that the followers of Christ who prayed "that they may all be one" (Jn. 17:21) are not one, but divided and in open competition; this is the greatest contradiction to the Gospel any reader will find in this book.

CONTENTS

Preface   *v*

CHAPTER ONE:
ECUMENICAL MARRIAGE   1

Mixed Marriage   2
  Ecumenical "Martyrs" • The Real Problem
Ecumenical Marriage   5
  The Non-Exclusive Nature of Baptism • Defining
  Ecumenical Marriage • The Necessity of Personal Faith
Pastoral Invitations   14
  Shared Communion
Summary Questions for Discussion   19
Suggested Reading   19

CHAPTER TWO:
ECUMENICAL MARRIAGE AS COVENANT   21

Covenant   22
  Levels of Meaning
Christian Marriage as Covenant   26
  To Sustain Equal Partnership • To Love One's Spouse
  as Oneself • To Nurture Discipleship
Summary Questions for Discussion   35
Suggested Reading   36

CHAPTER THREE:
ECUMENICAL MARRIAGE AS SACRAMENT   37

Prophetic Symbol   38
    Steadfastly Faithful
Sacrament   39
    More Than a Human Bond • An Impossible Ideal
Embodied Love   43
    The "Spiritualizing" Approach •Eros as God's Gift
Ecumenical Marriage: Sacrament to the Churches   49
Summary Questions for Discussion   50
Suggested Reading   51

CHAPTER FOUR:
DIVORCE AND REMARRIAGE   53

When a Marriage Dies   54
The New Testament on Divorce   54
A Test for Jesus   55
    Marital Exceptions
Roman Catholic Practice   59
Pastoral Practice Related
    to Divorce and Remarriage   61
    "A Spirit of Mercy and Forgiveness" • Conditions
    for Judgment • Grace Requires Faith
A Search for Clarity   69
Summary Questions for Discussion   69
Suggested Reading   70

CHAPTER FIVE:
PASTORAL CARE OF ECUMENICAL MARRIAGE   71

An Ideal World   72
Pastoral Task for the Whole Church   72
    Summoned to Serve
Ecumenical Education   75
The Promise of Children   78
    Religious Education: A Mutual Decision • A Call for
    Cooperative Preparation
The Canonical Form   83
Intercommunion   86
    Eucharistic Reconciliation • School for Scandal?
Summary Questions for Discussion   92
Suggested Reading   93

Afterword   95
Notes   97

Dedication

For Charles and Maureen,
Bill and Gail,
Peter and Anne,
and
All Such Sacraments to the Churches

CHAPTER ONE

∞

ECUMENICAL MARRIAGE

In November 1970, the Catholic bishops of the United States issued instructions for mixed marriages, marriages in which the spouses are of two different Christian faiths. They suggested that the personal efforts of mixed faith couples to achieve unity in faith are a participation in the broader efforts toward unity among the separated Christian churches. Ten years later, Pope John Paul II made the same point in his important exhortation, *On the Family*, proclaiming that "marriages between Catholics and other baptized persons...contain numerous elements that could be made good use of, both for their intrinsic value and for the contribution they can make to the ecumenical movement." He delineates what I shall later call "ecumenical marriages" when he goes on to assert that "this is particularly true when both parties are faithful to their religious duties."[1]

Mixed Marriage

Encompassing within one home the divisions among Christians, mixed marriages can be, like all Christian marriages, compelling signs and instruments of Christ's abiding love for the church, a love which seeks continually to reconcile. The religious agenda for couples in such marriages, the bishops and the pope suggest, is an agenda of loving reconciliation and healing of divisions between the spouses, as sign and instrument of reconciliation and healing of divisions between the churches.

When they accept two different faiths as validly Christian, the spouses in a mixed marriage offer an important witness to the divided Christian churches and to an equally divided world. While refusing to ignore the religious differences which divide them, they bear constant witness to the fact that the things that divide them are not nearly so important as the things that unite them—one love, one God, one Christ, one Spirit, one baptism. They bear concrete witness in their lives to the fact that mutual love, trust, respect, and a passionate desire to be united enable them to live and grow together in the midst of deep differences.

Ecumenical "Martyrs"   Because the Greek word for witness, *marturion*, is the root also of the English word *martyr*, we can say that spouses in a mixed marriage are both witnesses—and martyrs—for ecumenical unity. Martyr may seem too strong a word, in these "enlightened" times, but there are still couples who are "martyred" by apparently unloving and uncaring church bureaucracies. The churches, and the world in which they are called to be signs and instruments of love and reconciliation, can greatly benefit from their loving and reconciling "martyrdom." What the Roman Catholic *Code of Canon Law* proscribed in 1917 concerning mixed marriages exemplifies the attitudes of all the churches at that time: "The church everywhere most severely prohibits the marriage between two baptized persons, one of whom is a Catholic, the other of whom belongs to a heretical or schismatic sect. If there exists the danger of perversion of the Catholic spouse or child, the marriage is forbidden even by divine law" (Can. 1060). In this approach, a mixed marriage was viewed as a dangerous evil. The best way to deal with it, indeed the only way to deal with it, was to avoid it.

The Real Problem   A mixed marriage, however, as I have suggested, is not the real problem. The real problem the Christian churches face today, and choose largely to ignore, is not that a spouse of one Christian confession marries a spouse of another, but that there are different and competing Christian confessions.

In 1981, researchers Dean Hoge and Kathleen Ferry reported that the rate of mixed marriages for Catholics was about forty percent.[2] (Clearly the doom and gloom instructions of the churches about mixed marriages are being ignored by large numbers of Christians.) Some commentators suggest that in 1990 the number is closer to fifty percent. These facts, and the numbers associated with them, ought not to surprise us. Given the educational, economic and social mobility available, indeed almost prescribed, in North America, it is entirely predictable that men and women of different faiths will meet, fall in love and marry in greater numbers than ever before. Caring ministers of all Christian traditions, who know from pastoral (and sometimes personal) experience that a marriage needs no added tensions, agree that this situation demands a change in pastoral approach.

Instead of being simply prohibited or discouraged from committing themselves to a mixed marriage, those about to embark on one require and deserve the fullest preparation possible for it. Moreover, those already in one require and deserve pastoral support and nurture in their search to become "one body" (Gen. 2:24). The fact that such pre-"mixed-marriage" preparation is now offered by many churches is cause for Christian rejoicing—and widespread imitation. The fact that such post-marriage nurture continues to be unavailable, not only in mixed marriages but also in same-faith marriages, is a cause for great Christian lament. The words of John Paul II remain a clarion call: "The pastoral care of the regularly established family signifies, in practice, the commitment of all the members of the local ecclesial community to helping the couple to discover and live their new vocation and mission. In order that the family may be ever more a true community of love, it is necessary that all its members should be helped and trained in their responsibilities as they face the new problems that arise."[3]

My central point is that the traditional, and still to a large extent, negative approach of the Christian churches to mixed marriages—an approach which emphasizes only differences, problems, and dangers—is no longer useful when committed Christians of all confessions are intermarrying in such large numbers. In spite of the problems it shares with every other marriage, rooted in differences between the spouses and its special problems stemming from religious differences, a mixed marriage is as much a cause for celebration as any other Christian marriage. It is a gift, a grace and, in the words of Pope John Paul II, a contribution to the ecumenical movement.[4] A mixed marriage is a positive opportunity and challenge for Christian unity, both for the spouses who embrace it and for the Christian churches who bless it.

To underscore this positive approach, I reject in this book the term *mixed* marriage with all its traditional negative nuances and replace it throughout with a more positive term: *ecumenical* marriage. I realize that a change of language alone will not be enough to improve the churches' attitudes toward and pastoral care of ecumenical marriages. I suggest only that the effort to eliminate words, judgments and actions which do not correspond to the truth of the situation as perceived by believing Christians is a necessary first step. As the work progresses, I shall develop the notion of ecumenical marriage more fully.

Ecumenical Marriage

The introduction of the word *ecumenical* invokes a larger, more positive Christian context. The word derives from the Greek *oikumene*, the whole inhabited world. It refers, in traditional Christian usage, to a general council of the church and, in contemporary usage, to the search of the Christian churches for worldwide unity and communion. The cognate term, *ecumenical movement*, describes all those activities designed to promote that unity among Christians. My phrase, ecumenical marriage, is to be understood in this contemporary context. Two statements will serve to characterize this context. The first is from the Final Report of the Anglican Roman Catholic International Commission (ARCIC) in 1981: "From the beginning we were determined...in the spirit of Phil. 3:13, 'forgetting what lies behind and straining forward to what lies ahead,' to discover each other's faith as it is today and to appeal to history only for enlightenment, not as a way of perpetuating past controversy." Their final goal had been assigned to them four years earlier by the leaders of the two communions, the Archbishop of Canterbury and the Bishop of Rome. That goal was "the restoration of complete communion in faith and sacramental life," a goal which is "one with the sublime Christian vocation itself, which is a call to communion."[5]

The second statement is the canon on mixed marriages in the revised *Code of Canon Law* of 1983: "Without the express permission of the competent authority, marriage is prohibited between two baptized persons, one of whom was baptized in the Catholic church or received into it after baptism and has not defected from it by a formal act, the other of whom belongs to a church or ecclesial community not in full communion with the Catholic church" (Can. 1124).

Note the change in tone. Gone are the negative words and polemics of the earlier canon, the talk of perversion of the Catholic, the description of the non-Catholic as a heretic or schismatic. The negative statements are replaced by positive approval of the non-Catholic's baptism into and membership within a Christian church, a phrase which reflects Vatican II's momentous admission that there are other Christian churches besides the Catholic church. At least in theory, therefore, some negative judgments the churches held about one another are becoming more positive. I shall now explore the implications of a positive ecumenical climate in the special case of ecumenical marriage.

The Non-Exclusive Nature of Baptism   Baptism is not an exclusively confessional matter—an important theological fact which is frequently overlooked. No one is baptized exclusively into the Catholic church or into the Lutheran church or into the Orthodox church. They are baptized into the one, holy, catholic and apostolic church of Christ and of his God (cf. Acts 20:28; 1 Cor. 1:2; 11:22; 2 Cor. 1:1). In spite of intense pressure to repeat the teaching of Pius XII that the one church of Christ was identical with the "holy, catholic, apostolic, *Roman* church,"[6] the Second Vatican Council rejected that equation and taught instead that "this church...*subsists* in the Catholic church."[7] That is, this church is embodied in, but not identical with, the Catholic church. It is also embodied in, but not identical with, the Lutheran church, the Anglican church and the other Christian churches. While theologically it is true that each and every Christian today is inserted imperfectly into the church of Christ through the mediation of a specific Christian denomination, it is never to be construed that their baptism inserts them *only* into that denomination.

All the mainline Christian denominations accept today Vatican II's statement that those "who believe in Christ and have been properly baptized are brought into a certain, though imperfect, union with the Catholic church,"[8] as well as the Lutheran church, the Anglican church, and so on. They accept baptism in each other's church as baptism into the one church of Christ. This is why, therefore, they do not rebaptize anyone who transfers from one Christian confession to another. The degree of union between Christian believers of different confessions may not be perfectly clear in any given case, no more than it is clear within any given church. But it is quite clear that, in and through a shared baptism in the one church of Christ, believers of all Christian confessions share a unity as brothers and sisters in Christ. That foundational and theologically-based unity is of the greatest importance in an ecumenical marriage, and it should never be allowed to be forgotten or to be obscured by less foundational confessional differences.

Defining Ecumenical Marriage   What precisely do I mean

by the term *ecumenical marriage*? Unfortunately the definition proposed by the *Code* is imprecise. It is founded on an assumption that, sadly, is not verified today, either in the Roman Catholic church or in any of the other Christian churches. An anecdote from my experience of ecumenical marriage will enable me both to clarify this statement and offer a definition of ecumenical marriage confirming John Paul II's understanding: a marriage between two Christians of different confessions in which "both parties are faithful to their religious duties."

In the Preface you were introduced to my friends, Charles and Maureen, Bill and Gail. Though they do not seem to understand much about Catholic theology (perhaps even because they do not understand) Charles and Maureen take it for granted that their marriage is sacramental. That much, at least, they retain from a combined thirty-two years of Catholic education. They also take it for granted that the marriage of Bill and Gail is not sacramental, for it is not a Catholic marriage. Gail agrees with them, for her church does not consider marriage a sacrament. Though their language is not this sophisticated, the kind of debate they get into about their various points of view is well summed up by the *Final Report of the Roman Catholic-Lutheran-Reformed Study Commission on "The Theology of Marriage and the Problem of Mixed Marriages."*

The report, issued in 1976, notes that, "according to Catholics, the Reformation was particularly radical in its approach to the question of marriage." In the name of a doctrine of personal justification, the Reformation churches contested the doctrine of the Catholic church on marriage. The Catholic church, on her part, developed a doctrine of marriage as sacrament which was unacceptable to the Reformation churches. It appeared to them that the Catholic church sought to introduce in marriage "automatic" grace, which is theologically unacceptable and spiritually unverified. "In the view of Lutherans and the Reformed churches, the Catholic church, in holding that marriage is a sacrament, seems to forget that marriage does not of itself give grace but needs to receive it."[9] An examination of that statement will lead us to important conclusions about the marriages of both Charles and Maureen and Bill and Gail.

Charles and Maureen are mistaken on two counts. They are wrong, first, to assume that their marriage is sacramental simply because they are baptized Catholics. They are wrong, secondly, to assume that the marriage of Bill and Gail is not sacramental just because Gail is not a baptized Catholic. I shall deal with each of these two points in turn.

When I read the New Testament, even superficially, I am always struck by the insistence on the necessity of personal faith for salvation. Jesus complained insistently about the absence of faith, for example, and Paul passionately defended the necessity of personal faith against the Judaizers. The primacy of personal faith, a "comprehensive 'yes' to God revealing himself as savior in Christ,"[10] was acknowledged at the time of the Reformation by both the Reformers and the Catholic church. Martin Luther made "faith alone" one of his rallying cries. The Council of Trent (1545–1563), the centerpiece of the Catholic Reformation, taught that "we may be said to be justified through faith," citing the letter to the Hebrews in its support: "Without faith it is impossible to please [God] (11:6)."[11] There can be no doubt that, despite the post-Reformation polemics which tended to ignore and, therefore, obscure this common agreement, the primacy of personal faith for sanctification and justification is as much a Roman Catholic doctrine as it is a Protestant one.

The Council of Trent taught also that sacraments confer the grace they signify on those who present "no obstacle."[12] It opted for this basic formula to cover in one statement the case of both infants and adults, but it applies positively only to the case of infants. In the prior Ecumenical Council of Florence, the Roman tradition had already carefully specified that, for an adult, "placing no obstacle" meant having a positive intent. The sacraments give grace only to those who receive them worthily.[13] This doctrine demands a personal, active disposition of self-surrendering faith on the part of the one who participates in a sacrament. A sacrament, this doctrine declares, is a true sign of faith. It is a sign, that is, not only of the faith of the church which seeks to make explicit and to celebrate in sacrament the presence of God and of Christ, but also of the faith of believers who positively seek to acknowledge and to celebrate that presence with the church.

The Second Vatican Council reaffirms that position as the Catholic position. It teaches that sacraments "not only presuppose faith" but also "nourish, strengthen and express it." That is "why they are called 'sacraments of faith.'"[14] Catholic teaching is, and always has been, clear. Grace, the loving presence of God in Christ, is never automatic, not even in sacraments, not even in the sacrament of marriage. The gracious presence of God becomes effective for a believer, is "received" as imprecise theological language says, when the sacramental action is matched by the believers' internal disposition to accept it, their faith, their love, their comprehensive "yes" to the presence of God. It is only when the external action and the internal disposition come together that there is effective sacrament.

One of the most famous Catholic theologians, Thomas Aquinas, never doubted this. The saving action of God and Christ, he taught, "achieves its effect in those to whom it is applied through faith and love and the sacraments of faith."[15] Personal faith, the believer's present "yes" to God, the internal disposition that Aquinas and other medieval theologians called *opus operantis*, is as essential to the conferral of grace in and through sacraments as the most carefully crafted external action that they called *opus opera-tum*.

There is, therefore, a serious doctrinal flaw in the position of my friends Charles and Maureen, who believe that grace is "automatic" in the sacrament of marriage, and of the *Code of Canon Law* from which it derives. The revised *Code* still claims that "a valid marriage contract cannot exist between baptized persons without its being by that very fact a sacrament" (Can. 1055, 2). That means that in every case in which there is a valid marriage contract between baptized persons (note that the *Code* does not say baptized *Catholic* persons) there is valid sacrament. That statement is true as a statement of the faith of the church. The natural reality of marriage, created by the mutual consent of the spouses, is offered by the church as also a sacrament of the union between it and Christ. It is accepted as sacrament, however, and as, therefore, grace-full only by those who personally share the faith of the church.

The Necessity of Personal Faith No one is graced and justified without personal faith, not even in sacraments. The longstanding teaching of the Roman Catholic church that sacraments are essentially "sacraments of faith" insists that they place men and women in the context of explicit grace only when the external sacramental action and their personal belief coincide. Charles and Maureen, and everyone else who believes that grace is automatic in the sacrament of marriage, are quite wrong. Their marriage is not automatically sacramental just because they are baptized Catholics. If it is sacramental at all, it is not just because they are Catholics but because they are *believing* Catholics, who share the faith of their church that the universal human reality called marriage can be also a sacrament of the presence of the gracious God. A sacrament is an encounter with God, and there is no possibility of one-sided encounter.

Charles and Maureen are wrong also when they assume that the marriage of my other friends, Bill and Gail, is not a sacrament because Gail is not a baptized Catholic. The Roman Catholic church does not doubt, and never has doubted, that the marriage between any two baptized believers can be as sacramental as the marriage between two Catholic believers. The *Code of Canon Law* is merely repeating a long Catholic tradition when it legislates that "a valid marriage contract cannot exist between *baptized* persons without its being by that very fact a sacrament" (Can. 1055, 2). What is required for the marriage of Bill and Gail to be sacramental is exactly the same as what is required for the marriage of Charles and Maureen (two "cradle" Catholics) to be sacramental.

Bill and Gail, just like Charles and Maureen, must accept in faith the sacramental action offered by the church, in this case their marriage, as an effective sign of the presence of the loving God in whom they say they believe. The marriage of Bill and Gail can be as sacramental as the marriage of Charles and Maureen, if they want it to be. If pastors would instruct both prospective and actual ecumenical spouses on the sacramentality of their marriage and, therefore, on the very positive situation of grace and Christian holiness offered them by their marriages, they would be of infinitely more help to them in their married and religious lives than all the canonical prohibitions of the past.

Gail, of course, never thinks of her marriage as a sacrament for the simple reason that she is a good Presbyterian. The Reformer John Calvin (1509–1564), whom she always cites in the crunch, defined sacrament as a sign instituted by Christ for the whole of the faithful. Marriage does not meet that definition; only baptism and the Lord's Supper do. Marriage, therefore, is not a sacrament and is not to be thought of as such. It is as simple as that.

Gail, however, needs to take account of another of

Calvin's teachings on marriage. Though he does not agree with the Catholic church that marriage is a sacrament, he does agree that marriage is a sign of the covenant, modeled upon the union of Christ and the church. All the Reformation churches have followed him in this teaching, and the Second Vatican Council committed the Catholic church to this same position.[16] Gail needs to consider, as do all of us, that while the language of the Catholic and the Reformation traditions is different, the situation of grace reflected in the language may be quite similar. When it comes to the presence and effectiveness of grace, it is not Christ that divides Gail and Bill, but the different languages of their churches.

I shall explore in greater detail the notions of covenant and sacrament, and their interrelationship, in the chapters that follow. Here, however, I shall simply provide a summary message to Charles and Maureen, Bill and Gail, and the many couples of similar religious backgrounds.

All Christian churches emphasize the central importance of personal faith in the process of justification and of sanctification. Non-believers, even if they happen to be *baptized* non-believers, are not graced in and through the sacrament of marriage or any other sacrament—not because of the inefficacy of grace or marriage or any other sacrament, but because of their lack of faith. All the churches are burdened today with people known as "baptized non-believers," people whom they count as believers simply because they have had water poured on them. The marriages of these non-believers, whether Catholic or ecumenical, are not sacraments. I thank God for all of you are believers and, therefore, capable of transforming your marriages into sacraments if you want to.

It is critical to note that all marriages in which one spouse is described as belonging to one Christian confession and the other spouse as belonging to another not be lumped together in a single category. There are, as I see it, three possible categories, specified by the faith or non-faith of the partners. There is the category in which neither partner is committed to any Christian confession, the category in which only one partner is committed, and the category in which both partners are committed.

An ecumenical marriage, as I have defined it and as I use the term throughout this book, is one in which the spouses share a common Christian faith in one God, one Christ, one Spirit, and one baptism. It is a union in which spouses grow together in that faith, though each in good conscience belongs and intends to continue to belong to a different Christian church. This is what I mean by "ecumenical marriage." This category of Christian marriage can become exemplary for all other types of "mixed" marriages, and I thank God for the wonderful example my friends, Bill and Gail, who have provided a truly ecumenical marriage.

Pastoral Invitations

Bill, like countless others in similar marriages, will want to know the implications of what I am saying. It is not helpful to respond that those implications will be developed as we go along, for that future promise, I know from experience, is unsatisfactory. Here, therefore, I will set out the implications. (They *will*, however, recur and be developed in more depth as we go along!)

First, I invite all Christians to think about the marriage of Bill and Gail not as a *mixed* marriage, and therefore a source of only dangers and problems, but as an *ecumenical* marriage, and therefore as a gift and challenge to the unity of all Christians. All the Christian churches like to call the Christian family a "domestic church,"[17] a little church which is the most common image and representation of the universal church of Christ. As believing members of a little ecumenical church, Bill and Gail can achieve a unity that is doubly rooted. It is rooted, first, in their marital covenant to become one body (Gen. 2:24); it is rooted, secondly, in their baptismal covenant to become one Christ (Gal. 3:27–28).

The loving unity ecumenical spouses can achieve out of these twin roots exceeds the unity achieved by the members in any Christian congregation, and far exceeds the unity achieved between any of the churches. The reconciliation, the healing of divisions, the mutual love and trust and respect achieved in ecumenical marriages, despite the different confessions of the spouses, is a gift to all of us and a challenge for us to achieve the same.

Second, I invite all Christian spouses to recognize the sacramental character of their marriages, ecumenical and Catholic alike. For Catholic spouses, that will be easy, though they should never take their faith or the sacramentality of their marriages for granted. For Protestant spouses, like proudly Presbyterian Gail, it will not be so easy. I invite them, therefore, to recognize the covenantal character of their marriage. Though their churches do not agree that Christian marriage is a sacrament, they do see it as a covenant, modeled upon, and therefore also sign of, the covenant union between Christ and his church. That both a Protestant and Catholic spouse see their marriage as not merely a *social* reality but also a *religious* one offers them yet one more solid basis on which to build a viable personal and religious unity.

When an ecumenical family, a domestic ecumenical church, lives as a sign of the covenant between Christ and his church, it becomes also an instrument of that covenant. It becomes a sign and an instrument for all of us and all our churches of the presence of both Christ and the God he reveals. That presence is what the Christian traditions intend primarily in the word *grace*. A sign and an instrument of grace is, of course, precisely what the Catholic church means by sacrament. Because your marriage is a sign and an instrument of grace, of the loving presence of God in your married life, everything you do in it—your mutual trust, your mutual respect, your mutual service, your mutual love, including your sexual love—places you in the presence of the invisible God. It makes you holy. For all Christians, marriage is the primary setting for their obedience to their Lord's call to love their neighbor, their spouse, and their children as themselves.

Third, I invite all Christians to work at understanding one another's beliefs, not just the beliefs we are supposed to hold, but the beliefs we truly do hold. Spouses who love one another totally must seek to understand and appreciate one another totally, and must seek to educate their children totally. In ecumenical marriages and, perhaps, given the high rate of ecumenical marriages even in same-faith marriages, that education should be totally ecumenical. Such an education is the only human way to dispel the historical myths that still keep Christians apart.

Though the Catholic church still requires that Catholic spouses promise to do all in their power to rear the children of their marriages as Catholics, it also acknowledges that the education of the children in an ecumenical marriage is the mutual right and responsibility of both parents. The faith of both parents, and specifically the depth of their understanding of it, is a critical factor in the religious education of the children. Both parents in an ecumenical marriage must strive to understand as fully as possible the faith each brings to the marriage, so that the children can talk freely to both parents. This precludes the divisive prospect of a child consulting one parent for information on one faith and the other parent for information on the other.

Fourth, I invite all Christians to acknowledge without defensiveness or mistrust that ecumenical families should, at least occasionally, worship God together. Common prayer is a vital part of every Christian family. It is an even more vital part of an ecumenical family. For an ecumenical family, the old Christian adage "The family that prays together stays together," is especially true. It is not enough that their private family worship be together, as it is frequently in the case of Bill and Gail. Their public worship, the communal celebration of the liturgical prayer of every Christian and every Christian family, must also be performed together on a regular basis. It needs also to include, at least occasionally, the sharing of communion if they so desire.

Shared Communion This question of shared communion is one that is hotly and emotionally debated in the churches. But the Christian unity achieved between ecumenical spouses, every bit as much as the unity achieved between same-faith spouses, demands ritual celebration in the great Christian meal of communion. Their two churches have celebrated and blessed their oneness in Christ in baptism and their oneness in love in marriage. They ought not to use the central Christian ritual of the Lord's Supper to drive a wedge into that unity, certainly not in the case of ecumenical spouses as I have defined them. Such a strategy is an unforgivable assault upon the ecumenical family. On this point, I agree with theologian James Mackey: "Any 'officer' who prevents Christians from participating in a eucharist celebrated by another Christian church, especially when the best theological endeavors have shown the same faith in Christ's real presence in both churches, is not only acting *ultra vires*, he is actively propounding a false view of Christianity."[18]

My friends Bill and Gail have often told me of their

spiritual need and desire to celebrate and promote their oneness in shared communion. I am suggesting only that their need is serious enough for their two churches to respond to them pastorally by offering them the Christian hospitality of shared communion. That hospitality is presently permitted by the Catholic church in cases of serious need. It is an open secret that it is already practiced with, at least, tacit episcopal approval in Catholic and Protestant dioceses all over the world.

Finally, I invite all Christians to remember our common Lord and what he stands for in our world. Mark's Jesus announces that he came "not to be served but to serve" (10:45). No Christian church, Catholic or Protestant or ecumenical, should be less than a church of service. Like all Christians, therefore, spouses in an ecumenical family are called to a discipleship of service. They are called to serve one another, their families, their two churches and the other communities in which they live. They are called most especially to serve other ecumenical families, by sharing with them and by sustaining them with their lived ecumenical experience and insight.

Their Christian service is one more gift and challenge ecumenical spouses offer to their divided churches, one more sign that people who differ can still live together in mutual love and trust and helpfulness. Since it is not only a sign but also an instrument of the goal of complete communion, enunciated twenty years ago by the Archbishop of Canterbury, head of the Anglican church, and the Bishop of Rome, spiritual leader of Roman Catholicism, ecumenical marriage is also a sacrament of that communion. The goal of complete communion, I hope all will agree, coincides with the goal of Christianity itself: "That they may all be one" (Jn. 17:21).

Summary Questions for Discussion

1. Do you think that substituting *ecumenical marriage*, and the attitudes associated with it, for *mixed marriage*, and the attitudes associated with it, makes any real difference?
2. What have you been taught about Christians in other traditions? What are your attitudes toward other Christians and toward the ecumenical movement? What are your attitudes toward Christians who commit themselves to ecumenical marriages?
3. What does it mean to say that Christian marriage, ecumenical or not, is sacramental? Does it make any difference in your married life?
4. If you had to make the decision about which Christian denomination the children of an ecumenical marriage would be reared in, how would you set about making that decision?
5. How would you feel about a Christian from another denomination receiving communion in your church? Why?

Suggested Reading

Abbott, Walter M. *The Documents of Vatican II* (London: Chapman, 1967). See especially "The Decree on Ecumenism," pp. 341–366, and "The Constitution on the Church," pp.14–96.

Faithful to Each Other Forever: A Catholic Handbook of Pastoral Help for Marriage Preparation (Washington, D.C.: United States Catholic Conference, 1989).

Hoge, Dean, and Kathleen M. Ferry. *Empirical Research on Interfaith Marriage in America* (Washington, D.C.: United States Catholic Conference, 1981).

Meyer, Harding, and Lukas Vischer. *Growth in Agreement* (Mahwah, New Jersey: Paulist Press, 1984).

CHAPTER TWO

∞

ECUMENICAL MARRIAGE AS COVENANT

Marriage is defined by the Second Vatican Council as an "intimate partnership of married life and love...rooted in the conjugal covenant of irrevocable personal consent."[1] This doctrine enables us to construct a preliminary description of Christian marriage. It is a community of life and love, founded in a mutual and permanent covenant by which a Christian man and a Christian woman give and accept one another to establish an intimate, life-long partnership.

Covenant

The word *covenant*, which we have encountered already as both a Protestant and a Catholic way to speak of Christian marriage, is not randomly chosen here. It is an ancient theological word, conjuring up for Christian spouses biblical images of both the great covenant between Yahweh and Yahweh's people and the extension of that covenant in the new covenant between Jesus and his people. In the Roman Catholic church it is also a new canonical word, replacing in the 1983 *Code of Canon Law* the long-established legal word *contract*. Reflection on the distinctive nuances of contract and covenant will introduce us to crucial changes which have taken place in Catholic teaching on marriage.

Covenant is clearly a more biblical word than contract; it is also a more personal word. Contract bespeaks mutual rights and obligations; covenant speaks of mutual personal gifts. Theologian Paul Palmer has attempted to clarify the meanings of covenant by contrasting it with contract:

> Contracts deal with things, covenants with people. Contracts engage the services of people; covenants engage persons. Contracts are made for a stipulated period of time; covenants are forever. Contracts can be broken, with material loss to the contracting parties; covenants cannot be broken, but if violated, they result in personal loss and broken hearts. Contracts are secular affairs and belong to the marketplace; covenants are sacral affairs and belong to the hearth, the temple or the church. Contracts are best understood by lawyers, civil and ecclesiastical; covenants are appreciated better by poets and theologians. Contracts are witnessed by people with the state as guarantor; covenants are witnessed by God with God as guarantor. Contracts can be made by children who know the

value of a penny; covenants can be made only by
adults who are mentally, emotionally and spiritually
mature.[2]

These distinctions need to be not only read but also pon-
dered. They enable us not only to distinguish covenant
from contract but also to name a most significant change in
the twentieth-century Roman Catholic approach to marriage. It has become more person-oriented.

"The beginning, the subject and the goal of all social in-
stitutions," the Second Vatican Council teaches, "is and
must be the human person, which by its very nature
stands completely in need of social life."[3] Marriage, the intimate community of life and love, the mutual self-giving
of a man and a woman, is a social institution and therefore
exists for the human person, as Vatican II suggests in its
person-oriented choices.

These choices include: the use of the word *covenant*
(rather than the word *contract)* to describe marriage; the
description of the formal object of marriage as the mutual
gifting of the spouses themselves one to another (rather
than the traditional giving and accepting of just their bodies);[4] and the insistence that the mutual conjugal love of the
spouses is equal with procreation as an end of marriage
(rather than a secondary end as had been traditionally
viewed).[5] These choices broadcast, and were intended to
broadcast, that marriage has more to do with personal and
human, rather than biological and legal, realities. The fact
that these choices were made public only after intense de-
bates in the Council and reproduced in the same form
twenty years later in the new *Code of Canon Law* attests that
they were not accidental.

The description of marriage as covenant links it to the
two model covenants in the Christian tradition: the great
covenant between Yahweh and Yahweh's holy people and

the new covenant between Jesus and his holy people. Chronologically, perhaps even logically, there is, first, the great covenant; then there is the extension of this great covenant in the new covenant; and, finally, there is the covenant of Christian marriage which is an extension of and a participation in both.

Levels of Meaning   In every symbol, there are two levels of meaning. There is a foundational level and, built on this foundation, a symbolic one. On the foundational level, for instance, water produces both life and death, which makes it apt to express on the symbolic level meanings of death and resurrection, as it does in the Christian symbol of baptism. Christian marriage has the same two levels of meaning. On the foundational level, there is the community of life and love between a Christian man and a Christian woman. On the symbolic level, rooted in this foundation and quite inseparable from it, there is the reflection and representation of the community of life and love between Christ and his church.[6] In other words, Christian marriage proclaims and celebrates, on a foundational level, the mutual love and fidelity of the spouses. On a symbolic level, it proclaims and celebrates the mutual love and fidelity of Christ and his church. This two-tiered meaning is one reason the Catholic church teaches that Christian marriage is sacramental.

In Christian marriage, the symbolic meaning takes precedence over the foundational meaning, in the sense that the abiding love of Christ and his church is the model for the mutual love of the spouses. Christian spouses are not just a wife and a husband covenanted to one another, they are also the church in microcosm covenanted to their Lord—Vatican II calls them "the domestic church."[7] If it is to be Christian in any sense, that church is called to participate in the great church's covenant with Christ. When it does, it is graced. Christ and the God he reveals are present in it, gracing the spouses with their confessed presence, and providing them with models of abiding love.

Christian marriage, as I have explained, does not automatically effect grace. Nothing created automatically effects grace, which is "God himself in his forgiving and divinizing love."[8] Because grace is the loving and forgiving presence of God in human history, that history is a history of grace offered to every man and woman coming into the world. Since, however, not all men and women always acknowledge and celebrate the gracious presence of God, history is not always a history of grace accepted. To be actually graced, men and women have to *make grace*, in much the same sense as they have to make love.

To be graced, men and women consciously have to acknowledge, celebrate and respond in some symbolic action to the presence of God in their midst. Christian sacraments, however, are not the only ways to do this. When the Catholic church teaches that sacraments cause grace, this is all it means. The imaging of Christian marriage as covenant has been traditionally a Protestant approach; the Catholic tradition has imaged it more as sacrament. The covenant approach emphasizes interpersonal relationship founded in the consent of the spouses. The sacramental approach, on the other hand, emphasizes the abiding bond which, though initiated by the consent of the spouses, continues to exist until the death of one of the spouses, even if their consent to be married is withdrawn. Belief in that abiding bond, of course, leads the Catholic church to deny the possibility of remarriage after a divorce. I hope to demonstrate that the two approaches are not so different as they might seem or as they have been made out to be. However, we must first ask: What are the implications, both theoretical and practical, of saying that Christian marriage is a covenantal relationship?

Christian Marriage as Covenant

To form a covenant is to commit oneself radically and solemnly. When a man and a woman establish a covenant in Christian marriage, they commit themselves mutually to a life of equal and intimate partnership in abiding love. They mutually commit themselves to creating and sustaining a climate of personal openness, acceptance, trust, and honesty. They commit themselves to rules of behavior which will respect, nurture and sustain intimate community and abiding love. They commit themselves to exploring together the religious depths of human life, and therefore of married life, and to respond to those depths in the light of their Christian faith. They commit themselves to abiding in love and in covenant, and to withdrawing from the covenant only when the life of intimacy has ceased to exist and available means to restore it have been tried and have failed.[9]

In Christian marriage, a man and a woman commit themselves to creating a life of equal and intimate partnership in abiding love. When the Lord Yahweh made the heavens and the earth, when no plant had yet sprung up from the land because the Lord Yahweh had not yet brought forth rain, a mist went up from the earth and watered the ground. The mist, of course, turned the dry earth to mud, in Hebrew 'adamah, and from that 'adamah the Lord Yahweh formed 'adam and breathed into her and his nostrils the breath of life. And 'adam became a living being (Gen. 2:4–7). "When the Lord Yahweh created 'adam, he made 'adam in the likeness of Yahweh. Male and female he created them, and he blessed them and he named them 'adam" (Gen. 5:1–2).

This parable, for it is indeed a parable and not a scientific or historical description, provides those who accept it with an answer to a perennial question: Where did we come from? We, in English, *humankind*, in Hebrew, *'adam*, came from God. Male and female as we are, we are from the Lord Yahweh, and together we make up humankind or *'adam*. This fact alone, that Yahweh names man and woman together as *'adam*, establishes the equality of man and woman as human beings.

The further parable, which speaks of the creation of woman from the man's rib, intends in the original Hebrew to emphasize man and woman's equality, not their separate creation. In their recent pastoral response to the concerns of women in the church, the Catholic bishops of the United States underscore this fact. Since "in the divine image...male and female (Yahweh) created them" (Gen.1:27), woman and man are equal in human dignity and favor in Yahweh's eyes. They are equal in everything that is human; they are "bone of bone and flesh of flesh" (Gen. 2:23). It is only because they are equal, says the parable, that woman and man may marry and "become one body" (Gen.2:24).

As Western Christians have seriously misunderstood the Hebraic myth about equal man and woman, *'adam*, so also have they misunderstood the Hebraic understanding of becoming one body. They have linked it much too exclusively to a single facet of becoming one in marriage; namely, the joining of bodies in sexual union. This facet is undoubtedly part of what is involved in becoming one body, but it is far from all that is involved.

In the original biblical myth, "body" does not refer to the external, physical part of the human being, as it does in English. It refers rather to the whole person. In marriage, therefore, a man and a woman enter not only into a sexual union, in which their physical bodies are made one, but also into a personal union, in which their entire persons are made one. Marriage, in the biblical myth, is for the good of the human person in a very special way. Marriage in the Jewish culture of Jesus' time differed greatly from marriage in contemporary American culture.

In the Americas, individuals marry and enter into a relationship which society guarantees as a legal relationship. In Jesus' culture, families married and the spouses entered into a relationship which society guaranteed as a blood relationship. In that blood relationship, they become one body, one person, in a way that quite escapes the understanding of anyone who thinks only in physical and legal terms. They became, as the Lord Yahweh intended them to be, equal man and woman, complementing one another to form again, one 'adam. Rabbis have long taught that, according to God's design, neither man nor woman is whole until each receives the complement of the other in marriage.

The notion of equal partnership and community in which spouses covenant themselves in Christian marriage is captured well by a contemporary United Methodist statement on marriage. It affirms "the sanctity of the marriage covenant, which is expressed in love, mutual support, personal commitment and shared fidelity between a man and a woman." It confesses that "God's blessing rests upon such a marriage, whether or not there are children of the union." And finally, it rejects "social norms that assume different standards for women than for men in marriage."[10] Such an intimate and equal partnership of married life and love is not the result of a developing women's liberation. It is the demand of the founding myth in which Christianity is rooted.

To Sustain Equal Partnership The covenant of marriage is a mutual commitment not only to create a life of equal partnership, but also to nurture and sustain it. Again, the Hebrew tradition in which Christian reality is rooted gives the lead. Psalm 136 is a hymn of praise to Yahweh's abiding love. It makes clear that the commitment of Yahweh to create *'adam* and the world in which she and he live is a commitment also to sustain *'adam*. "Give thanks to Yahweh, for he is good, for his abiding love endures forever...to him who spread out the earth upon the waters, for his abiding love endures forever" (Ps. 136:1, 6). The images of covenant in the Christian tradition are of commitment not only to create but also to sustain what one has created. Yahweh is not a God who creates and then leaves creation to fend for itself, just as Jesus is not a Christ who gives himself up for the church (Eph. 5:25) and then abandons her. In the same way, the genuine followers of Yahweh are not men and women who create a marriage of equal partnership and then leave it to survive by itself.

For the covenant of marriage to be sustained, conditions must be created which will constantly nurture it. When a man and a woman form a covenant in Christian marriage, therefore, they commit themselves mutually to create rules of behavior which will nurture and sustain the marriage. For genuinely believing Christians, those rules are found by paying careful attention to their tradition.

The letter to the Ephesians provides scriptural rules for the living out of the marriage covenant. Its author provides a list of traditional household duties performed in first-century Palestine. He critiques the cultural assumption of inequality in this list, and instructs all Christians to "give way to one another because you stand in awe of Christ" (5:21). This critique challenges the absolute authority of any Christian individual or group over another, including husbands over wives. It establishes the basic attitude required of all Christians, even when they are married—an awe of Christ and a "giving way to one another" because of it.

As all Christians are to yield to one another in certain circumstances, it is hardly surprising that a wife is to give

way to her husband, "as to the Lord" (5:22). But the instruction given to husbands is surprising, at least to those
husbands who see themselves as the lord and master of
their wives and who appeal to the letter to the Ephesians
to support this attitude. The instruction is not that the husband is the head of the wife, which is the preferred male
reading, but that "the husband is the head of the wife *as*
(that is, in the same way as) Christ is head of the church"
(5:23). An obvious question arises: How does Christ act as
head of the church? The writer gives the equally obvious
answer: "He gave himself up for her" (5:25). It is a vibrant
echo of a self-description that Jesus offers in Mark's Gospel: "The Son of Man came not to be served but to serve"
(10:45).

The Christian way to exercise authority is to serve. Jesus constantly pointed out to his power-hungry disciples
that in his kingdom the leader is the one who serves (Lk.
22:26).

Christlike headship is not absolute control of another
human being; it is not making decisions and passing them
on to another to carry out; it is not reducing another human being to the status of a slave. To be head as Christ is
head is to serve. The Christian head is called always to be
the servant of other persons. As Markus Barth puts it so
beautifully, the Christian husband-head becomes "the first
servant of his wife,"[11] and she becomes his first servant.
One rule of behavior for the nurturing and sustaining of
the covenant of Christian marriage is the rule of mutual
service.

The letter to the Ephesians embraces one other rule for
behavior in Christian marriage, a great Jewish and Christian commandment: "You shall love your neighbor as
yourself" (Lev. 19:18; Mk. 12:31). Husbands are instructed
that they "should love their wives as their own bodies"
(5:28a), and that the husband "who loves his wife loves

himself" (5:28b). We can assume this instruction, which reflects the Genesis account of man and woman's creation out of the same body, is intended also for a wife.

To Love One's Spouse as Oneself The Torah and Gospel injunction to love one's neighbor as oneself applies in Christian marriage. The rules of Christian behavior that will respect, nurture and sustain the covenant and the community of ecumenical marriage are easy to summarize: love one's neighbor-spouse as oneself, with a love which is yielding, abiding, and characterized by mutual service. A paraphrase of Paul sums it up even more succinctly. Those who love their spouses have fulfilled all the rules of behavior in a Christian marriage (cf. Rom. 13:8).

What the writer of Ephesians concludes about the one-body image of Genesis 2:24, that, "This is a great mystery, and I mean in reference to Christ and the church" (5:32), will lead us into the consideration of the sacramental depth of human existence in general and of marriage in particular. The mystery is, as the Anchor Bible translation seeks to show, that this passage refers to Christ and the church. The writer is well aware that this is not the meaning given to the text in traditional Judaism, and states forthrightly that it is a personal reading of the text, "*I* mean in reference to Christ and the church."

Genesis 2:24 was an excellent text for the purpose the writer had in mind, for it was the central Torah text traditionally used to ordain and legitimize marriage. The author acknowledges the traditional understanding that a husband and wife become one body or blood person in marriage and, as we have seen, demands that a Christian husband and wife live up to this meaning. But goes beyond this meaning.

On one level, Genesis 2:24 refers to the covenant union of a man and a woman in marriage; on another level, it refers to the covenant union between Christ and his church. It is a small step to perceive the union between a man and a woman in marriage as a symbolic representation of the union between Christ and his church. The Orthodox churches make this step by celebrating Christian marriage as a mystery; the Catholic church makes it by celebrating it as a sacrament.

A Christian marriage is not just a wedding ceremony to be celebrated. It is also a loving and equal partnership of life to be lived. When establishing a covenant in ecumenical marriage, Christian spouses commit themselves to exploring together the religious depth of their existence, and responding to that depth in the light of affirmations about it that are central to the faith of Christians.

One of the most central affirmations of ecumenical Christian faith is the affirmation of discipleship. "Disciple" is an omnipresent New Testament word, always implying response to a call from Jesus. Disciples, by definition, are learners, and the disciples of the Christ are learners of mystery. They gather together in response to his call to explore a triple mystery: the mystery of the one God who seeks to be known and to be loved by them; the mystery of the Christ in whom this God is embodied and revealed; and the mystery of the church in which they gather, which is the Body of Christ (Eph. 1:22–23; Col. 1:18, 24). Since the covenanted family is a little, domestic church, the spouses in it are called to be learners of these mysteries and of their implications for married life.

Marriage does not separate the spouses from life. It immerses them in life and confronts them with the ultimate questions of life and death that are the stuff of religion. There are questions about joy in love and the birth of children; about pain in illness and suffering and alienation; about fear, grief, and isolation, and death; about happiness in friends and beauty and success. Marriage demands that sense be made out of these and a thousand other confusing questions. Christian marriage, ecumenical or non-ecumenical, demands that sense be made of these questions in the light of the shared Christian faith of the spouses.

To Nurture Discipleship As they find adequate Christian responses to the demands their married life imposes on them, Christian spouses mutually nurture one another in Christian discipleship. They learn and grow together in Christian maturity. The more they mature, the more they come to realize the ongoing nature of being married and being a covenant sign. They come to realize that, though their marriage is already *a* sign of the covenant between Christ and his church, it is not yet the *best* sign it can be. For the best sign to emerge from their marriage, takes time. In Christian marriage (a life of Christian discipleship), even more than in secular marriage, the answer to the age-old question of when two people are actually married is simple: thirty, forty, perhaps fifty years after they first exchanged vows.

Spouse-disciples in a covenant marriage are required to learn one thing above all others—what their common commitment to God stands for in a sinful, divided, broken world. The answer lies, in part, in Jesus' assertion that he had come "not to be served but to serve" (Mk. 10:45). Any Christian, individual or couple or church, can be nothing less than for others. The little, domestic church which is the Christian family can be, similarly, nothing less than a church of service, reaching out responsibly to the various communities in which it subsists.

It is fashionable to associate this ethic of social responsibility with the Puritans, but this association misses an important point. Social responsibility *is* a Puritan ethic, but it is a Puritan ethic only because it is first a Christian ethic. Service to the society in which they live is the responsibility of all Christians, unmarried and married alike. Marriage adds only the specification that Christian spouses are called to exercise their service in the context of their married life. Ecumenical spouses, therefore, are called to exercise it in the context of their ecumenical married life.

We can conclude this chapter, then, as we began it, with a definition, only now a more fully elaborated one. Christian marriage is an intimate partnership of life and love, the origin of which is in God's creative act and in the covenant of the spouses' mutual consent, and the goal of which is to give glory to God by shaping the religious and moral life of the spouses in imitation of the Christ. That this definition is ecumenically Christian can be seen from the prayers of two contemporary marriage services.

First, the exhortation to the spouses in the Presbyterian service, which I first experienced at the wedding of Bill and Gail, invites them to be "merciful in action, kindly in heart, humble in mind." It instructs them to "accept life, and be most patient and tolerant with one another. Forgive as freely as the Lord has forgiven you. And, above everything else, be truly loving. Let the peace of Christ rule in your hearts." It concludes with that most ancient of Christian exhortations: "Never forget to be thankful for what God has done for you."[12]

Secondly, the nuptial blessing in the Catholic service prays over the spouses. "Father, keep them always true to your commandments. Let them be living examples of Christian life. Give them the strength which comes from the Gospels so that they may be witnesses of Christ to others."[13] If its ritual prayers are always the best interpreter of the meaning of a Christian service, and they are, there can be no doubt about the Christian meaning of covenant marriage.

The marriage services of all the Christian churches underscore also their common conviction that, when a man and a woman mutually form a covenant in marriage, they commit themselves to abide in love and in covenant as long as life lasts. I share this common Christian conviction. I take it to be self-evident that the covenant of Christian marriage creates a moral obligation to be faithful to the mutual commitment it implies. That is, after all, what covenant and love mean. Covenant creates a relationship in which I am bound to keep my word; love by its very nature tends to be lifelong. The problem is that some marriages do not last as long as the life of the spouses. They cease to be; they die. The problems this creates for the Christian churches will be dealt with in Chapter Four.

Summary Questions for Discussion

1. What does it mean to you to say that Christian marriage is a covenant? Is a covenant both an image of and a participation in the covenants between God and God's people and between Christ and his church?

2. What are your thoughts about the Genesis story of the creation of woman from 'adam's rib? Does it tend to emphasize the equality of man and woman as human rather than their separate creation?

3. What rules would you offer for nurturing and sustaining the covenant of ecumenical marriage?

4. How do you see the covenant of ecumenical marriage as enabling spouses to grow together in an ongoing way as disciples of Christ?

5. In your opinion, how can ecumenical spouses best serve the Christian churches and the other communities in which they live?

Suggested Reading

Lawler, Michael G. *Secular Marriage, Christian Sacrament* (Mystic, Connecticut: Twenty-Third Publications, 1985).

Palmer, Paul. "Christian Marriage: Contract or Covenant?," in *Theological Studies* 33 (1972), pp. 617–665.

Yates, Wilson. "The Protestant View of Marriage," in *Journal of Ecumenical Studies* 22 (1985), pp. 41–54.

CHAPTER THREE

∞

ECUMENICAL MARRIAGE
AS SACRAMENT

Religions are always on the lookout for images of God and
of God's relationship to the human world. In the Jewish
prophets, we find an action image, known as the prophetic
symbol. Jeremiah, for instance, buys an earthen pot, dashes
it to the ground and explains to a crowd of onlookers what
he is doing. "Thus says the Lord of Hosts: so will I break
this people and this city, as one breaks a potter's vessel"
(19:11). Ezekiel takes a sharp knife, shaves his hair with it
and divides the hair into three bundles. One bundle he
burns, another he scatters to the wind, a third he carries

around the city and shreds even further with his knife. In prophetic explanation of his actions, he proclaims: "This is Jerusalem" (5:5).

Prophetic Symbol

Each prophet clarifies the radical meaning of his actions, which also clarifies for us the meaning of a prophetic symbol. As Jeremiah shattered his pot, as Ezekiel cut and burned and scattered his hair, so God shatters and scatters and burns Jerusalem. The depth meaning and reality symbolized by Jeremiah is not the shattering of a cheap clay pot, but the shattering of Jerusalem and of the covenant relationship between Yahweh and Yahweh's people. The prophetic symbol is a representative action, an action which proclaims, makes explicit and celebrates in representation some other, more fundamentally meaningful reality.

Since the idea of their special relationship to Yahweh arising out of their mutual covenant was so central to the self-understanding of Israelites, it is easy to see why they would search out a human reality to symbolize the covenant relationship. It is equally easy, perhaps, to see why they chose the human covenant of marriage.

The prophet Hosea appears to have been the first to speak of marriage as the prophetic symbol of the covenant.

On superficial appraisal, the marriage of Hosea and Gomer is like any other marriage. Hosea advanced it, however, as a prophetic symbol, proclaiming, making humanly explicit and celebrating in representation the covenant relationship between Yahweh and Israel. Just as Gomer left Hosea for other lovers, Israel left Yahweh for other gods. Moreover, just as Hosea waits for Gomer to return to him, so also Yahweh waits for Israel.

Hosea's human action is a prophetic symbol, a representative image, of God's abiding love in spite of every violation. Hosea's action proclaims, makes explicit and celebrates not only Hosea's faithfulness to his marriage covenant, but also Yahweh's faithfulness to the covenant with Israel.

Steadfastly Faithful One basic meaning about Hosea and Yahweh is clear: Hosea and Yahweh are steadfastly faithful. Yet there is another clear, if mysterious, meaning about marriage. It is also a religious and prophetic symbol proclaiming, making explicit and celebrating in the human world the abiding, if somewhat shaky, union of Yahweh and Yahweh's people. From this perspective, and pursued in faith, marriage becomes the kind of two-tiered reality referred to in Chapter Two. On one level, it bespeaks the covenantal love of this man and this woman; on another, it represents and symbolizes the covenantal love of Yahweh and Yahweh's people. First articulated by the prophet Hosea, this two-tiered view of marriage becomes the Christian view of marriage that is, as I've suggested, found in the letter to the Ephesians.

"This is a great mystery (in Latin, *sacramentum*) and I mean in reference to Christ and the Church" (Eph. 5:32). The great mystery or sacrament is that the text of Genesis 2:24, "and they become one body," a text that was traditionally read in relation to the union between a man and a woman in marriage, now is read in relation to the covenant between Christ and the church. Jewish prophetic symbol is transformed into Christian mystery and sacrament.

Sacrament

In the preceding chapter, we noted that the classical Protestant approach to Christian marriage views it as a sign of the covenant, while the classical Roman Catholic approach views it as a sacrament. To appreciate such categorizations, we need to understand the definitions on which they depend.

John Calvin defined sacrament as a sign instituted by Christ for the whole of the faithful. The Lutheran church offers a similar definition: a sacrament is an action of the church enjoined by Christ to be enjoyed by all Christians. Since only baptism and eucharist were so instituted and enjoined, the Reformation churches believe, they are the only rituals acknowledged as sacrament.[1] Though marriage is a sign of the covenant, it is not a sacrament. The classical Roman Catholic definition, is that a sacrament is an outward sign of inward grace instituted by Christ. While this definition was expressed by the Council of Trent, it took a thousand years to be established. In that time, all sorts of realities, including Christian marriage, floated in and out of the sacramental picture until the definition became universally accepted in the Catholic world.[2]

We are now in a position to offer a fuller explication of that classical definition. A sacrament is a prophetic symbol in and through which the church, the Body of Christ, proclaims, makes explicit and celebrates in representation that presence of God it calls grace. We shall gain insight into that definition as we explain how the graceful God is made explicitly present and celebrated by Christian believers in a Christian marriage.

We can and must distinguish two prophetic symbols in marriage. The first is the wedding ceremony, which ritualizes the giving and receiving of the consent "by which a man and a woman by an irrevocable covenant mutually give and accept one another for the purpose of establishing a marriage."[3] The second symbol is the married life of the couple, which concretizes their consent in a life-long and intimate partnership of married life and love. In street language, both these actions are called *marriage*. In theological language, they both deserve to be called *sacrament*. Both are sacraments of the mutual love and of the mutual partnership between God and God's people and between Christ and Christ's church.

To say that Christian marriage is a sacrament is to say that it is a prophetic symbol, a reality that has two tiers. On one tier, it proclaims and makes explicit and celebrates the intimate community of life and love between a Christian man and a Christian woman. On another, deeper tier, the religious and symbolic tier, it proclaims and makes explicit and celebrates the intimate community of life and love between Yahweh and Yahweh's people and between Christ and Christ's people, the church.

More Than a Human Bond Those entering into any marriage say to one another before the society in which they live: "I love you and I give myself to and for you." A Christian couple entering into a Christian marriage says that too, of course. But they also say much more. They say "I love you as God loves God's people and as Christ loves the church." From the first, therefore, their marriage is more than just the union of a man and a woman; it is more than just a human covenant. It is also religious covenant. God and Christ are partners in it from the beginning, modeling it in their union with people and church, gracing it, and blessing it.

The presence of grace in its most ancient Christian sense, namely, the presence of the gracious God, is not something extrinsic to the covenant of Christian marriage. Rather it is something essential, something without which it would not be *Christian* marriage at all. Christian marriage clearly proclaims, makes explicit and celebrates the mutual and abiding love of the spouses. It also proclaims, makes explicit and celebrates their abiding love for their God and for the Christ they confess as Lord. It is in this sense that it is a sacrament, both a sign and an instrument, of the presence of Christ and of the gracious God he reveals. We already learned from our reading of the letter to the Ephesians that the love between a husband and a wife in Christian marriage is not just any love. It is love that loves one's neighbor (read one's spouse) as oneself. It is love which gives way to the other, love which is mutual service, love which is faithful and life-long. Such a love is not difficult to promise in a wedding ceremony, but is difficult only to deliver over the long-haul of a married life. Christian marriage, like all Christian sacraments, embraces both the ceremony and the life *after* the ceremony.

The claim that marriage is a life-long sacrament is a lofty one. But it is the claim the Catholic church makes when it affirms that the marriage of two Christian believers, Catholic or not, is a sacrament. It is also the claim two Christians make when they profess they are entering into a *Christian* marriage. For most of us married couples, it is a claim that is extraordinarily difficult to live out, because it is extraordinarily difficult for a man and woman, socialized to become thoroughly *in*dependent individuals, to become one, *inter*dependent, "blood" person. While this is a challenge in any Western marriage, it is an enormous challenge in an ecumenical marriage, in which the spouses, on top of everything else, are divided on the basis of deeply-held religious convictions.

An Impossible Ideal   I do not believe that becoming one blood person (in Hebrew, "one body") promotes the impossible and perhaps undesirable, ideal that a husband and a wife should agree about absolutely everything. It does intend that each of them should come to understand their own feelings, needs and desires on the three levels on which they seek to live—the animal, the human and the religious—and that neither should ever treat the other as anything less than a full partner. All *exclusive* self-love, which is not the same thing as legitimate self-love,[4] is excluded by a "one-body" relationship. (If spouses are to grow, both individually and mutually, they need to learn legitimate self-love.)

Universal history demonstrates how unity between two human beings is always threatened by exclusive selfishness and the desire to remake another person in one's own image. A marriage that seeks to become a one-body marriage, however, must strive for such unity. Unless it does, it remains at best an inadequate symbol of the one-body unity between Christ and his church. It remains, at best, only imperfectly sacramental.

It is precisely because of the difficulties involved in becoming one body that Christian marriage is an essentially eschatological symbol. That is, although it is already a prophetic symbol and sacrament of the covenantal union between Christ and the church, it is not yet the perfect symbol it needs to be. This "already-but-not-yet" dimension of Christian marriage is both a comfort and a challenge. It is a comfort to the extent that Christian spouses can claim in truth that their marital union is both modeled upon and model of the union between Christ and his church. It is a challenge to the extent that Christian spouses must confront constantly their falling short of, and their need to become more attuned to, their model.

Embodied Love

In the previous chapter, I noted that the marriage covenant does not withdraw spouses from life but, rather, immerses them in it. So too with sacrament. The intercourse between a husband and a wife in every aspect of their married life is sacramental. Each and every aspect of their lives places them explicitly in the loving presence of God and of the Christ whom they confess as Lord.

The great teacher of the Catholic tradition, Thomas Aquinas (1225–1274), explains that the marital intercourse between spouses takes place on three levels: the animal, the human and the religious.[5] Our discussions thus far have been limited to the religious and human levels of that intercourse. It is time now to say a word about the "animal" level—the level of physical and sexual intercourse in a one-body marriage. That word must be a word of *reverse discrimination*, not because the physical is all there is to life in marriage, but because it is an essential part of married life, even of Christian married life, and it has historically suffered from a strong ambivalence and negativity among the various confessions of Western Christianity.

When the early Christian church was driven out of its Jewish cultural homeland, it was forced into dialogue with the Greco-Roman culture and with the philosophies that dominated it. I shall briefly mention only two of them, Gnosticism and Manicheeism, for though great Fathers of the Church, such as Clement, Irenaeus, and Augustine, responded to these doctrines by teaching that sexuality and marriage, as creations of the good God, are necessarily good, a very negative attitude toward sexuality and its use in marriage crept into Christianity from these Greek sources.[6] That negative attitude can still be detected today in Catholic theology and in the continuing effort to spiritualize sexuality.

Gnosticism taught a very pessimistic and dualistic view of the world, in which good and evil are equally real, and in which matter is essentially evil. As matter, sexuality and marriage are evil and, in the normal outcome of sexual intercourse, contribute to evil matter in the world. They are, therefore, to be avoided by anyone seeking a higher, more spiritual life. Manicheeism, an equally dualistic system, also taught that sexuality and marriage are evil and, therefore, to be avoided.

The "Spiritualizing" Approach What I have called the "spiritualizing" approach to human sexuality and physical intercourse attempts to locate their value exclusively on the spiritual level of human existence. A man and a woman, such an approach argues, "encounter" one another, "communicate," and "make love" through their sexuality. I do not object to saying that men and women do such human and spiritual things through their sexuality; I agree that they do. What I object to is saying that is *all* they do. It is not what the spiritualizers include that bothers me but what they exclude. I have the same objection to the spiritualizing approach as that articulated by theologian John Giles Milhaven: "Man does do these spiritual, personal things in his sexual life (encounters, communicates, expresses love, etc.), and they do constitute the principal value of human sexuality, but not solely. The bodiliness and sexualness with which he does them changes intrinsically their nature and therefore their value from what they would be in a nonbodied, nonsexual person's life."[7] Man and woman are not disembodied spirits; their encounter, their communication, their making love, and their other spiritual interaction are essentially embodied activities. There is no way to banish the body from the human. To locate human sexuality exclusively on the spiritual level of personal existence is every bit as much a betrayal of the human as to locate it exclusively on the animal level.

It is not at all difficult, however, to understand the mainspring of such an approach. The elements of the human that lie on the non-spiritual level, especially on the animal and physical level, are precisely those elements that Christians have been socialized to distrust. To become one body, however (and I make no apology for returning to this in a discussion of the meaning of Christian marriage), Christian spouses must come to terms with all their needs, feelings and desires on all three levels of their existence, including the much maligned animal level. Becoming one blood person includes becoming not only one spirit, not only one mind, but also one physical body.

Married love is undoubtedly *agape*, the love of the spouse for the spouse's sake; but it is also more than *agape*. It is undoubtedly *philia*, the love of the spouse as a friend; but it is also more than *philia*. It is undoubtedly *eros*, the love of the spouse for one's own sake; but it is also more than *eros*. Because it might appear strange to some to read in a book about Christian marriage that marital love is also *eros*, the love of the spouse for one's own sake, I hasten to put it another way. Marital love is loving your neighbor *as yourself* (Matt. 22:39).

Since Augustine of Hippo (354–430), the Christian commandment to love one's neighbor as oneself has been recognized in the Catholic tradition as the foundation for a wholly justifiable self-love. Such self-love is very much in evidence when two people are well along the way to becoming one body, for in such a marriage *both* spouses have become mutually full and fully esteemed personal partners and not just objects. In such a marriage, "I love you" matures into "I love me and you," and ultimately, as Milhaven puts it so beautifully, "we love us."[8] One does not have to have been long in marriage counseling to come to understand that a universal reason why so many men and women have difficulty coming to love another human being is that they have great difficulty ever coming to love themselves.

Eros **as God's Gift** So back to *eros*, that rambunctious, non-rational, selfish, much-maligned and over-exploited component of human sexuality and human love. The spiritualizers always wince at its very mention, and seek to transform it into *agape*. There is, however, no alchemy to effect such a transformation. *Eros* is an intrinsic, and therefore inescapable, quality of human love. Men and women, therefore, have to accept it, to integrate it, and to give it a distinctively human form. That distinctive form, I suggest, is created by harnessing the power of *eros* to the power of human wisdom. By definition, *eros* is the love of another for one's own sake. If *eros* dominates my love for my spouse, I trample another human being and use her exclusively for my own ends. That approach, perversely, leads to the very situation it seeks to avoid, namely, isolation, loneliness, unlovedness. If wisdom dominates, I recognize that my spouse's happiness is the only way that I too can ultimately be happy. Wisdom does not transform *eros* into *agape;* it simply allies itself with it. Such an alliance allows marital love to continue when all the things that fuel *eros*—youth, beauty, grace, form, passion—have long since passed away.[9]

Sexuality, sexual passion, sexual pleasure, *eros*, derive their spiritual and sacramental character, in the first instance, not from any spiritualized meaning we assign to them, but from the simple theological fact that they are from God. They are God's creation gifts to *'adam;* they are, so to speak, God's wedding gifts to a man and a woman. And they are good gifts. When they are used as good gifts in the process of becoming one in Christian marriage, they are used in a way that points to their origin in God. That is already to use them mysteriously and sacramentally, in a way that is not only physical and personal and spiritual but also religious and grace-full.

Physical union, as I have attempted to demonstrate, is not all there is to a Christian marriage. But it is an essential part of both such a marriage and its sacramentality. If

Christian marriage is a prophetic symbol of the covenant between God and God's people and between Christ and Christ's church, then the physical union achieved in sexual intercourse is an integral part of that symbol. In other words, sexual union in marriage proclaims, makes explicit and celebrates not only the physical, personal, and spiritual union between the spouses but also, the God who is grace and who is present to the spouses in this physical, human and prophetic action. That God is the same God who did not shrink from proclaiming steadfast love in that most beautiful and erotic of love songs, the Song of Songs.

The language of the song is explicit. "I am sick with love," the woman exclaims (2:5; 5:8). "Come to me," she cries out to her lover in desire, "like a gazelle, like a young stag" (2:17; 8:14). When he comes and gazes upon her naked form, he is ecstatic. "Your rounded thighs are like jewels, the work of a master hand. Your vulva is a rounded bowl that never lacks mixed wine. Your belly is a heap of wheat, encircled with lilies. Your breasts are like two fawns, twins of a gazelle" (7:1–3). Her reply is direct. "I am my beloved's, and his desire is for me. Come, my beloved, let us go forth into the fields....Let us go out early to the vineyards....There I will give you my love" (7:10–12).

Such obviously erotic language has long posed problems for interpreters of the song. Unwilling to consider that human, erotic love could have any place in the word of God, many have opted for an allegorical reading. The Song of Songs, they piously explained, is about divine love. But men or women who have ever been sick with love cannot mistake the language or doubt its meaning.

If the song is about spiritual, non-erotic love, it is so only secondarily. It is primarily about erotic love, about love that at least includes *eros*, about love that is joyfully sick with passion and desire. It is about the love of a man and a woman, who seek not only the bodily presence of each oth-

each other but also bodily union. This love is celebrated as gift, and therefore image, of the Creator God and of God's love for humankind. It is celebrated, therefore, as good and worthy to be included in God's word, to honor not only the giver but also the gift and the men and women who use it to make not only human but also "divine" love.

Ecumenical Marriage: Sacrament to the Churches

The ecumenical family is not just any domestic church, it is also an *ecumenical* domestic church. If it succeeds in becoming a united ecumenical church, it becomes a living example of what such a church could be. It becomes both a sign of an ecumenical church to the institutional churches, and an instrument through which they too can come to Christian unity. A sign and an instrument, as I have noted, is all Catholic theology means by sacrament. The ecumenical family is, therefore, a sacrament of Christian unity for the churches.

The opening section of this book called attention to the religious agenda set for ecumenical marriages in 1970 by the Catholic bishops of the United States. That agenda called for reconciliation and healing of divisions between the spouses, as sign and instrument of reconciliation and healing of divisions between the churches. When they accept as valid two different Christian faiths, ecumenical spouses bear witness to the simple fact that the many things that divide them are not nearly as important as the one love, one baptism, one God, one Christ, and one Spirit that unite them. Both the Christian churches and the world in which they are called to be symbols of love and reconciliation and peace stand in great need of such a loving sacrament.

In every committed marriage, the spouses take their separate beliefs, separate habits, and separate pasts, and from them try to fashion shared beliefs, shared habits, and a shared future. In committed ecumenical marriages, such shared beliefs happen to include different Christian beliefs, and, from these, spouses try to fashion a shared Christian life. The differences remain as painful signs that the domestic ecumenical church is no less and no more sinful than the divided institutional churches. As it struggles steadfastly to become one, to become holy, to become apostolic, to become catholic (which is never to be confused with *Roman* Catholic), the domestic ecumenical church serves as a sign and an instrument, that is, as a sacrament, of those same realities in one, holy, apostolic and catholic, ecumenical church.

The churches owe such a sacrament, such a light to the nations, the best possible and extended pastoral care. Each of them already has in place strategies for preparing people for ecumenical marriages. But they have developed those strategies in isolation from one another, and often in open opposition one to the other. It is time for the churches to agree on unified and cooperative pastoral care. It will be no easy task to overcome their traditional negative approaches to mixed marriages. But overcome them they must if they are ever to provide Christian nurture for the sacrament of ecumenical marriage that their common Lord has raised up in their midst.

Summary Questions for Discussion

1. What do you understand by the term *prophetic* symbol? Compare its meaning to that of three other symbols in your life.

2. What does it mean to you to say that Christian marriage is a prophetic symbol? Does this make Christian marriage something quite different from non-Christian marriage?

3. What do you understand by the statement: Christian marriage, ecumenical or otherwise, is a sacrament? What implications does this have for your married life?

4. Is it easy or difficult for you to think of sexual intercourse as an integral element of the sacramentality of marriage? Why? Is it really possible, as the Catholic church teaches, that sexual intercourse in marriage is a source of grace for the spouses?

5. How do you understand the claim that an ecumenical marriage is not only a sacrament of the presence of God, but also a sacrament of reconciliation and unity to the churches? Do you agree that ecumenical marriage can be such a sacrament?

Suggested Reading

Haughton, Rosemary. *The Theology of Marriage* (Notre Dame: Fides, 1971).

Lawler, Michael G. *Symbol and Sacrament: A Contemporary Sacramental Theology* (Mahwah, New Jersey: Paulist Press, 1987).

Roberts, William P. *Marriage: Sacrament of Hope and Challenge* (Cincinnati: St. Anthony Messenger Press, 1983).

Thomas, David M. *Christian Marriage: A Journey Together* (Wilmington: Michael Glazier, 1983).

CHAPTER FOUR

∞

DIVORCE AND REMARRIAGE

The marriage services of all the Christian churches underscore their common conviction that, when a man and a
woman mutually covenant in marriage, they commit themselves to abide in love and in covenant as long as life lasts.
I share this Christian conviction. I take it to be self-evident
that the covenant of Christian marriage creates a moral obligation to be be faithful to the mutual commitment it implies. For that is what both covenant and love mean. Covenant creates a relationship in which I am bound morally to
keep my word; love by its very nature tends to be life-long.

When a Marriage Dies

Some marriages, however, do not last as long as life; they cease to be; they die. The Christian churches are as divided about the proper pastoral approach to such failed marriages, and to the remarriages which frequently follow them, as they are united in their conviction about the life-long nature of marriage. Since these divisions are serious for both churches and spouses, they deserve serious examination. I propose such an examination here.

My point of departure will be, first, a consideration of the words of Jesus on divorce and remarriage, on which the different pastoral actions of the churches claim to be based, and, secondly, the too-easy assumption that what the Catholic church teaches is that the obligation deriving from the marital commitment is absolute, and that such teaching derives from Jesus. I propose to show that the New Testament teachings on divorce and remarriage are not as uniform as we might like them to be, and that the assumption about the teaching of the Catholic church is too simplistic and does not match its traditional practice.

The New Testament on Divorce

The synoptic Gospels report the position of Jesus toward divorce and remarriage four different times: in Mark 10:11–12, Matthew 5:32 and 19:9, and Luke 16:18. In his first letter to the Corinthians, 7:10–11, Paul also reports a prohibition of divorce and remarriage and attributes it to the Lord. Each of these reports requires close attention.

Mark is the first Gospel to be written, some forty years after the death of Jesus. The Gospel is written so tradition holds, for a Hellenistic Christian community. In the passage in question, Pharisees come to Jesus "in order to test him" and ask whether it is lawful for a man to dismiss his wife.

Jesus replies that, though Moses commanded divorce, it was not so from the beginning when God made male and female. "For this reason a man shall leave his father and his mother and be joined to his wife, and the two shall become one flesh. So they are no longer two but one flesh. What therefore God has joined together let not man put asunder (10:7–9)." Later, "in the house," the disciples ask Jesus about the same matter. He explains to them that "Whoever dismisses his wife and marries another commits adultery against her. And if she dismisses her husband and marries another, she commits adultery" (10:11–12).

The last sentence, though apparently innocuous and obvious to Western minds, is important, for it confirms that the audience for which Mark is writing is a Hellenistic one. In the Hellenistic world of Jesus' time, both a wife and a husband could initiate divorce proceedings. Just as their free consent had married them, so their free withdrawal of consent unmarried them. In the Jewish world of first-century Palestine, however, the notion that a wife could divorce her husband was unheard of under normal circumstances and was, therefore, something which a Jewish Jesus would probably never have said to a Jewish audience. The point to be grasped here is that Mark has no qualms about interpreting the Jewish saying of Jesus for his Greco-Roman audience.

A Test for Jesus

The Pharisees set out to test Jesus' allegiance in an ancient Jewish dispute. The Book of Deuteronomy describes the ground for divorce in Judaism. That ground is "something shameful" (*erwat dabar*), the precise meaning of which was and is hotly debated in Judaism. The great Rabbi Shammai and his disciples interpreted *erwat dabar* narrowly; it meant some serious sexual delinquency. The equally great Rabbi

Hillel and his disciples interpreted it broadly; it included not only serious sexual delinquency but any delinquency whatsoever, including the burning of the family porridge.[1]

The test to which Jesus is subjected here is to see if he would side with either Hillel or Shammai, thereby alienating the adherents of one camp. But he refuses to take sides, choosing rather to direct the argument back to the beginning described in Genesis. He argues that God's will from the beginning was that a man and a woman be joined in marriage in such a way that they become one body, "one person" in Hebrew. How, then, could a man dismiss his very own person in a divorce?

Jesus' argument is clear. Marriage, as intended by God in the beginning, is to be life-long and indissoluble. "What, therefore, God has joined together let not man put asunder" (10:9). He then explains to the disciples "in the house" what it all means, indicating that "whoever divorces his wife and marries another commits adultery against her" (10:11). Matthew has two versions of this saying of Jesus, both of which restate Mark's parable with a significant addition. "Whoever divorces his wife, except for *porneia*, and marries another, commits adultery" (19:9; cf. 5:32). Jesus' saying about divorce and remarriage would have been clear were it not for Matthew's exceptive clause, except for *porneia*, found neither in Mark nor in Luke. The meaning of the exceptive clause has been as endlessly debated as the meaning of its Hebrew equivalent, *erwat dabar*. It seems to me pointless to rehash that debate here yet once again.[2] I wish, rather, with the majority of scholarly opinion, to underscore quite a different point—that the exceptive clause was added by Matthew for his own purposes (as was his wont with the sayings of Jesus). Matthew, like Mark, fully aware of Jesus' saying on divorce and remarriage, did not hesitate to interpret it in the light of the specific circumstances of the community out of which he wrote.

Neither did Paul.

Paul's first letter to the Corinthians, written some fifteen years before any of the Gospels, answers questions posed to him by the Jesus community at Corinth. In response to a question about divorce, he reaffirms the Lord's command: "To the married I give charge, not I but the Lord, that a wife is not to be separated from her husband. And if she is separated, she is to remain unmarried or is to be reconciled to her husband. And a husband is not to dismiss his wife" (7:10–11).

There was a specific case of conscience about divorce and remarriage which must have been as common in Corinth as it is today in mission territories. The case is this: What about the divorce, and the subsequent remarriage of the spouses, in a marriage in which one spouse has become Christian and the other has remained non-Christian? Paul has two separate bits of advice for spouses in such marriages, each of them hinging on the attitude of the non-Christian spouse.

Marital Exceptions   If the non-believing spouse is willing to continue to live in the marriage with a Christian, then she or he is not to be dismissed. The Lord's saying holds firm: "What God has joined together let not man put asunder." If the non-believing spouse, however, is unwilling to live with a Christian, and if he or she wishes to leave the marriage, then he or she is to be allowed to do so. There is no suggestion that the marriage in this case is not a valid marriage. There is no suggestion that the Lord's saying does not apply to it. There is only the suggestion that, in this special case, Paul is making an exception ("I say, not the Lord" [7:12]).

The reason he offers for the exception is that "the brother or sister is not to play the slave in such matters. For God has called us to peace" (7:15). For Paul, in a hierarchy of truths, peace and harmony between spouses apparently stands higher than the legal bond of marriage. It is as interesting a reason now as it was then. As I shall discuss later, the Roman Catholic church sanctioned this approach to dissolving the bonds of valid marriages in the twelfth century and continues to sanction it today.

It should already be clear that we ought not to speak of the New Testament *teaching* on divorce and remarriage as if there were one uniform message. In reality, there are several *teachings*, and they are far from uniform. Nor are they derived solely from Jesus. There is a well-remembered saying of Jesus, the original form of which, by common agreement, is "Everyone who divorces his wife and marries another commits adultery" (16:18). But "if this is what Jesus said," anthropologist Bruce Malina argues convincingly, "it has to be a parable," a conclusion which is supported by the fact that "in the Gospels of Matthew and Mark this teaching requires further, private explanation, a procedure these authors use for parables."[3] If it is a parable, then it requires interpretation for application in the concrete circumstances in which hearers may find themselves. Interpretation for specific, concrete circumstances is precisely what the New Testament writers provide.

Mark adds to Jesus' Jewish saying the prohibition that a wife is not to dismiss her husband, something that would simply have baffled Jesus' Jewish audience. Matthew, good Jew that he was, adds an exception to Jesus' saying—except for *porneia*—whatever that meant to him and to his community. Paul adds his own exception for specific missionary cases.

The approach of these varied and sainted writers to Jesus' saying places theologian Theodore Mackin's judgment beyond gainsaying: "Because every element of the instruction on divorce and remarriage is part of the Gospel (and this includes the instruction in 1 Corinthians, even that part coming from Paul himself), it would falsify our reading of this Gospel if we were to single out one element, play it off against the others and make it override them."⁴ Divergent accounts of Jesus' saying on divorce and remarriage, as of several other sayings, are an integral part of the New Testament tradition.

There are divergent accounts, we now believe, because there were different Christian communities with different questions. Mark, Matthew, and Paul provided concrete answers for concrete questions relating to divorce and remarriage in specific communities of Christians, Jewish-Christian or Hellenistic Christians. The Roman Catholic church followed, and continues to follow, their lead by providing concrete answers to much the same concrete questions in its historical times. We shall now consider that Roman Catholic practice.

Roman Catholic Practice

The Catholic church has long agreed with the vast majority of moralists that the obligation deriving from commitment is limited, not absolute, and can be withdrawn for a reason higher in the hierarchy of truths than is the marriage bond. (This is what I intended to suggest in Chapter Two when I asserted that, in the covenant that is Christian marriage, a man and a woman pledge mutually to abide in love and in covenant, and to withdraw that pledge only if the life of intimacy has ceased to exist and all available means to restore it have been tried.)

Though the Roman Catholic church's reading of Jesus' saying on divorce and remarriage leads it to consider all valid marriages as indissoluble, it does dissolve valid marriages. Or, in plainer, street language, it grants divorces. The most ancient of these divorce procedures is the one derived from Paul's letter to the Corinthians, and called, therefore, the Pauline Privilege.

The Pauline Privilege applies to the marriage in which one spouse has become Christian and the other, non-Christian spouse refuses to live in peace with the new Christian. In this case, Paul says, the Christian spouse "is not bound" (1 Cor. 7:15); that is, the spouse is freed from the existing valid marriage. The reason Paul gives for this exception to the Lord's command is interesting: "God has called us to peace" (7:15). Peace, it would appear, is one of those higher reasons that makes release from the marriage commitment possible. It is, as I have said, as interesting reason now as it was then.

For our present discussion, however, what matters most is that the Roman Catholic church sanctioned this approach to dissolving a valid marriage in the twelfth century, continues to sanction it today (cf. Can. 1143), and names it the Pauline Privilege. In the centuries that have elapsed since Paul, the church has also extended the Pauline Privilege into the so-called Petrine Privilege, by which valid marriages are dissolved on the authority of the Pope in favor of the higher good called faith (cf. Can. 1148–1150).

There is yet a third way to dissolve a valid marriage in the Roman Catholic church. According to ancient Roman custom, a marriage actually took place when a couple freely consented to marry. In northern Europe, however, a marriage took place when the couple engaged in their first marital sexual intercourse. Unable, or unwilling, to discriminate between these two points of view, the medieval church combined them and taught that marriage was *initiated* by consent and *consummated* by sexual intercourse. If after the giving of consent, which initiates a valid marriage, there is no sexual intercourse, then the valid marriage may be dissolved (cf. Can. 1142), or, in common English, a divorce may be granted.

These Roman Catholic divorce procedures have rarely caused problems for Christians, for only the specialists ever knew about them. The case is quite different, however, with the famous, perhaps now infamous, procedure known as annulment. Annulment is an entirely different procedure from dissolution. The latter dissolves marriages held to be valid, while the former declares that, because of some deficiency at the moment of giving consent, there never was a valid marriage bond between a given couple. Common folk, of course, usually skip over the technical differences of these procedures, or simply lump them all together. They know that annulment is granted today in the United States more commonly than ever before, indeed that the numbers of "marriages" being annuled has increased fiftyfold since 1980. These facts lead them to conclude that the Catholic church is talking out of one side of its mouth when it says that divorce is not possible and out of the other side when it grants divorces called annulment.

To understand Catholic practice intelligently, people need to know two things. First, while holding firm, together with all the Christian churches, to the belief that marriage is to be life-long, the Roman Catholic church does acknowledge that marriages do fail and it does grant divorces in certain cases. These divorces need to be called *divorces* and not deliberately vague *dissolutions*. Secondly, annulment is not one of those divorce procedures, but merely a declaration that, in a specific case, there never was a legally valid marriage.

Pastoral Practice
Related to Divorce and Remarriage

The breakdown of marriage is always a human tragedy, causing hurt and harm to the spouses, their children, their families, and their friends. When a marriage fails—and anyone in touch with human reality will know that marriages do fail—real people find real turmoil, anger and hatred in the very context in which they sought to find security, peace and love. It is for this reason, for the hurt and the harm it causes, that divorce is an evil in the human community and, therefore, forbidden by God.

Those who believe that divorce is evil because it is forbidden by God, and they are legion, miss this point entirely, putting the cart before the horse. Kevin Kelly points out, invoking the support of Aquinas, that "God is not offended by us except in so far as we harm ourselves and other people. Marriage breakdown and divorce is evil because of the human hurt and suffering caused by it. It offends God because people precious to him are being harmed and are hurting each other."[5]

Each time the Roman Catholic church dissolves a marriage, it is for a good judged to be higher than is indissolubility. For Paul in first-century Corinth, it was the good called peace. For Pope Pius XII in twentieth-century Rome it was the good called "the salvation of souls, in which both the common good of the religious society...and the good of individuals find due and proportionate consideration."[6] Some contemporary Roman Catholic theologians are asking today if the good of concrete Catholic individuals can find due and proportionate consideration in the situation of divorce and remarriage. They are even suggesting some possibilities in which it can.

First, there is the ancient practice of the Orthodox church, going all the way back to its most revered bishops, Basil and Chrysostom. While holding as firmly as the Roman church to the belief that the Gospel message presents a demand for indissoluble marriage, the Orthodox church also acknowledges that, in reality, men and women sometimes do not measure up to the Gospel. It recognizes that some marriages, even genuinely Christian marriages, do indeed end, and when that happens it makes no sense to insist that spouses are still bound together by an indissoluble bond. It seeks to deal in a pastorally compassionate way with the former spouses, even to the extent of permitting and blessing the remarriage of an *innocent* spouse. Though the practice of the Reformation churches is not identical to this Orthodox practice, it is similar.

"A Spirit of Mercy and Forgiveness" Protestant positions on the question of divorce have shifted over the centuries. It is only in our century that Protestant churches have acknowledged that, in certain specific circumstances, divorce can be a morally responsible Christian action. They acknowledge that marriage is intended to be life-long, and they never resign themselves to the inevitability of divorce. They acknowledge also, however, a fact which, they claim, can be easily ascertained, namely, that some marriages do cease to exist. When a marriage does cease to exist, they feel free to permit both a divorce and a second marriage. They feel free also to hope that the second marriage will achieve what was not achieved in the first marriage—a greater conformity to the mutual, servant love of Christ and the church and thus a more adequate sign of the covenant between them.

The Lutheran-Reformed-Roman Catholic Final Report, which I referred to earlier, calls attention to three Gospel bases for this approach: "1) the doctrine of the justification of the sinner; 2) a view of the Gospel which, over and above all its requirements, sees the need for a spirit of mercy and forgiveness; 3) an interpretation of the passage in Matthew as indicating a Christian tolerance of divorce." It goes on to point out what was indicated in my treatment of Catholic divorce procedures, namely, that "there is some support for this doctrine in certain facts in the history of the Catholic church."[7]

The Roman Catholic church, which, it must be remembered, has its own array of canonical processes to dissolve valid marriages, has never condemned the Orthodox practice. Even the hard-line Council of Trent, which had before it a proposal to condemn that Orthodox practice as contrary to the Gospel, explicitly refused to make such a statement. In 1980, among the propositions presented to the pope from the Synod of Bishops was one asking that the Orthodox practice be considered carefully for the light that it might shed on Roman pastoral practice. Fidelity to Jesus' prohibition of remarriage does not exclude pastoral provision for the spiritual welfare of those who have entered second marriages, which have become so stable that they cannot be broken without grave economic, emotional and spiritual harm to the parties involved.

There is another, ancient Catholic factor which comes into play in the discussion of divorce and remarriage. When a marriage case is settled by some marriage tribunal, either for dissolution or for annulment, it is said to be settled in the "external" or legal forum. But the Catholic tradition universally teaches that moral questions are not settled in the external forum, but in the "internal" forum. The internal forum is the forum of good faith and of good conscience. In the hierarchy of truths, again, the love of the God who graciously saves outranks ecclesiastical teaching. That teaching should be honestly and respectfully heard. But it is the love of God that is at the heart of a Catholic conscience where men and women are finally alone with themselves, their God, and their moral judgments.

A moral decision in the internal forum related to divorce and remarriage is reached like this. A legally divorced Catholic, whose first spouse is still alive and whose first marriage has not been dissolved or annulled by the church in the external forum, after careful consideration of all the facts of her case as she understands them, makes an honestly considered, practical judgment that in the circumstances involved in her case, she is morally free to remarry. When she acts on this judgment and actually remarries, the church can and does accept her decision of conscience as morally binding on her, cannot and does not consider her a sinner, and cannot and does not bar her from full participation in the Gospel life of the community of believers.

Conditions for Judgment Such a serious moral judgment, of course, will have certain conditions attached to it to ensure its validity. Moral theologians suggest the following: First, none of the available ecclesiastical solutions can be applied to the case in question. Second, the first marriage must be irretrievably ended and reconciliation must be impossible. (An uncontested divorce, refusal by one party to be reconciled, and obligations toward children in a second marriage are serious signs that a marriage has ended.) Third, obligations deriving from the first marriage must be accepted and reasonably discharged. (Adequate child support, alimony, property settlement, acceptance of any responsibility for the failure of the first marriage, are among such obligations.)

Fourth, obligations deriving from a second marriage must be responsibly accepted and discharged. (The stability of the second marriage over a period of years, the birth of children, and the genuine desire to participate in the full life of the church are all credible indications of sincerity). Finally, the desire to participate in the sacraments of the church must be motivated by genuine Christian faith. This faith should always be presumed to be present in those who are sincerely pained by being barred from full participation in the life of the church.

A moral decision in the internal forum is, of course, an extremely difficult decision to make. But, then, every genuinely moral decision, made after "due and proportionate consideration" of all the information that must be taken into account, is extremely difficult to make. To suggest, as some do, that an internal forum solution offers "cheap grace" is to ignore completely the anguish that goes into making a difficult moral decision. A much more compelling case can be made that it is the tribunals which provide "cheap grace." It is the tribunals which, by offering Catholics legal declarations which they take to be moral choices, free them from their personal obligation to make a due and proportionately considered decision in their own moral conscience.

The bottom line in a moral decision about divorce and remarriage is never someone else's counsel, be that someone pope or bishop or friend, but the couple's honest decision that they are free or not free to remarry without any legal declaration in the external forum. Pope Pius XII has taught clearly that conscience is "the most intimate and secret nucleus in man. It is there that he takes refuge with his most spiritual faculties in absolute solitude alone with himself and with his God." Conscience is "a sanctuary on the threshold of which all must halt, man, woman or child"[8]—or, it could be added, ecclesiastical institution.

All external forum solutions to the problem of divorce and remarriage in the Catholic church are offered on the basis of the lack of some reality canonically judged to be indispensable for a valid marriage. In the case of the Pauline Privilege, that lack is the absence of baptism in one of the parties, along with the lack of will to live in peace. In non-consummated cases, the lack is of the physical consummation of the marital oneness. All of these are absences of some reality required for the validity of *marriage*. Because it is clear from Roman Catholic history, however, that the only marriage which is absolutely indissoluble is one which is both sacramental and consummated, Catholic theologians today are asking about the lack of some reality integral to the nature of *sacrament*.

That kind of approach comes up against the teaching of the *Code of Canon Law*, which declares that "a valid marriage contract cannot exist between baptized persons without its being by that very fact a sacrament" (Can. 1055, 2). The *Code* makes this statement because it assumes that what is called in the theological tradition the "gift of faith" is given in baptism. This assumption appears to be quite false in our day, in which that anomalous group of so-called Christians known as *baptized non-believers*, has emerged.[9] These are people who, though having undergone a baptismal rite (usually in infancy), are non-believers as adults. Their lack of faith raises serious questions about the sacramentality of any marriage into which they might enter.

Grace Requires Faith   The reader will recall here our introductory discussion of the primacy of personal faith in the process of salvation, a primacy which was equally affirmed by the Protestant Reformers and by the Council of Trent. The Second Vatican Council reaffirmed this tradition, teaching that the sacraments of faith are so called because they "not only presuppose faith" but "also nourish, strengthen and express it."[10] It is thus clear that the charge that Catholic sacramental doctrine makes grace "automatic" is entirely misplaced.

The Catholic tradition remains clear: personal grace, even in a sacrament, presupposes personal faith. A believer comes to a sacrament personally sharing in the faith of the church, and with that personal faith transforms with the church ordinary actions and words into prophetic symbols and sacraments. That personal faith, what the medievals called *opus operantis*, is as essential to sacramental fruitfulness as the most carefully crafted sacramental action, which they called *opus operatum*.[11]

There is a serious doctrinal flaw, therefore, in the *Code*. To claim that consent makes marriage is true; there is no marriage, sacramental or otherwise, without consent. To claim that marriage, created by mutual consent, is transformed into sacrament is true as a statement of the faith of the church. To claim, however, that marriage is automatically transformed into sacrament just because a person has undergone a baptismal rite requires a major distinction. Those whose personal faith matches the faith of the church transform indeed marriage into sacrament; those who do not share the faith of the church do not. No one is graced or justified or saved without personal faith, not even in sacraments, not even in the sacrament of Christian marriage. As I emphasized earlier, sacraments are encounters with Christ and with God, and there are simply no such things as one-sided encounters.

A marriage entered into with free consent but no faith is still a marriage, for consent makes marriage (Can. 1057). But it is not a sacrament, for it is personal faith that makes a sacrament. The universal tradition of the Catholic church insists that, since it is not a sacrament, neither is it indissoluble. The assessment of personal faith is obviously difficult, but no more difficult than the assessment of free consent. If marriages can be annulled for lack of free consent, they can also be annulled for lack of faith.

As there are putative marriages which are clearly not valid marriages because the consent which was thought to initiate them was not adequately free, so also are there putative sacramental marriages which are not sacraments because those who entered them were not adequately faithfull. As marriages are annulled for lack of consent, so also can they be annulled for lack of faith. If lack of faith cannot be sufficiently proven in the external forum, it can certainly be known by the concerned spouses in the internal forum. That knowledge arms them with the Christian freedom with which Christ, in and through his Holy Spirit, has set them free (Gal. 5:1). That freedom allows them morally to decide to have their marriage dissolved, to act on that decision, and to remarry if they so decide.

A Search for Clarity

This chapter has sought to clarify for ecumenical spouses the teachings of their various churches on divorce and remarriage. To this end, it considered the New Testament teachings on divorce and remarriage, along with the historical, ecclesiastical practices associated with them. No essay as short as this one could hope to respond to every expectation or to say everything that needs to be and could be said about Christian marriages.[12] What has been said is offered as a path to insight, both theoretical and practical, with which the twentieth-century churches might respond to the pressing problem (some say the _most_ pressing problem) of Christian marriage and its serious instability.

As a Catholic theologian who knows how things change in my church, I am convinced that the practice of the Catholic church with respect to marriage, divorce, and remarriage will cause Catholic theory to change, just as it has already caused Protestant theory to change. Such a pattern of change has always characterized church teaching.

Summary Questions for Discussion

1. Do you think it is accurate to say that the Roman Catholic church never grants divorces? Do you see any difference between a divorce and a dissolution of a marriage? If you do, what is the difference?

2. What was your reaction when you read that the say-

ing of Jesus about divorce and remarriage "has to be a parable"? If it is a parable, what does that mean to you? If it is not a parable, which of the New Testament reports about it should the churches follow today? Why?

3. What is your opinion about the practices of the Reformation and Orthodox churches with respect to divorce and remarriage? Do those practices have any relevance today for the Roman Catholic church? Do you have any opinion about what the attitude of the churches should be toward those thousands of Christians who have been divorced and remarried?

4. How do you react to the statement of Pope Pius XII that conscience is "a sanctuary on the threshold of which all must halt, man, woman or child"? Have you ever made a moral decision of conscience? What difficulties, if any, did you experience in making it? Do you think that such a decision could be made in the area of divorce and remarriage?

Suggested Reading

Coleman, Gerald D. *Divorce and Remarriage in the Catholic Church* (Mahwah, New Jersey: Paulist Press, 1988).

Kelly, Kevin T. *Divorce and Second Marriage: Facing the Challenge* (New York: Seabury, 1983).

Lawler, Michael G. *Secular Marriage, Christian Sacrament* (Mystic: Connecticut: Twenty-Third Publications, 1985).

Preister, Steven, and James J. Young. *Catholic Remarriage: Pastoral Issues* (Mahwah, New Jersey: Paulist Press, 1986).

CHAPTER FIVE

∞

PASTORAL CARE
OF ECUMENICAL MARRIAGE

The questions we have looked at so far in this book, questions of covenant, of sacrament, of life-long marriage, are theological questions. In an ideal world, Christians of every confession would simply accept the doctrines of their various churches on these matters, and our task would be at an end. We do not, however, live in an ideal world. This fact is poignantly illustrated for Christians by the statistics that show that the divorce rate for Christian marriages in the United States, ecumenical or not, lags only slightly behind the national rate for all marriages.

An Ideal World

This final chapter, therefore, considers not theological questions about the abstract meaning of ecumenical marriage, but practical, pastoral questions of how to minister to ecumenical marriages. It seeks to provide positive directions to churches, congregations, pastors and ecumenical spouses so that all may nurture ecumenical marriages to their fullest Christian maturity.

Pastoral Task for the Whole Church

The Lutheran-Reformed-Roman Catholic Final Report insists, correctly, that pastoral care "for the needs of individuals and families is not the task of the pastor alone but is the responsibility of the whole church."[1] That statement, which derives from a very ancient view of the community of men and women called both church and the Body of Christ, may sound strange in ears accustomed to authoritarian structures. We begin, therefore, with a brief outline of a vision of church in which the statement would not be cause for surprise.

Church is a word commonly used by Christians, but not commonly understood. The first Christians used the ordinary Greek word *ekklesia*, the gathering of those called, to describe themselves, and it is from this word that we derive the meanings of the English word *church*. Christians do not merely *belong* to a church. They *are* a church, a people gathered together in the belief that God has raised Jesus of Nazareth from the dead (1 Cor. 15:4; Acts 2:24) and has made him Lord and Christ (Acts 2:36). They are a people so intimately united with one another, because they are intimately united with Christ and his God, that they cannot be separated into "Jew nor Greek...slave nor free...male nor female," but they are together only "one person in Christ Jesus" (Gal. 3:27–28). Church, then, is essentially communion, but also more than simple human communion. Church is, on the one hand, a communion of human believers with one another and, on the other hand, a communion of all of them with their common Lord. As such a two-tiered communion, it is a symbol, a sign and an instrument of the presence in the world of that Lord and of the loving God he reveals. It is communion that is, as the Second Vatican Council carefully taught, "a kind of sacrament."[2] To put all this in the traditional words of Western theology: as Jesus the Christ once incarnated the invisible God, so now does the church incarnate an invisible Jesus.

Summoned to Serve   Luke opens his account of the ministry of Jesus with a quotation from Isaiah: "The Spirit of the Lord is upon me, because he has anointed me to preach the good news to the poor. He has sent me to proclaim release to the captives, and recovering of sight to the blind, to set at liberty those that are oppressed" (4:18–19). Luke sees Jesus as possessing a strong sense of having been anointed and sent to preach the presence of the kingdom and to confront whatever might obscure that presence. He is anointed, however, as Mark is quick to point out, "not to be served but to serve" (10:45), and he leaves his followers in no doubt that this is their way too to greatness in God's kingdom (9:35). The mission of Jesus is a servant mission. The mission of the church, which is his people and his Body, can be nothing less.

Those who confess faith in Jesus are anointed in baptism to be *christos*, Christ.[3] If the Christian, that is, the anointed, church is to be a credible sign and instrument of the presence in the world of the servant Christ, each and every member will have to serve as the church is called to serve.

Becoming Christ demands more than ritual baptism. It demands a life lived in imitation of Jesus, the original servant Christ. Every man and woman who would aspire to be named *Christian* must heed Christ's invitation: "Follow me" (Mk. 1:17). The pastoral care of individuals and families is not, therefore, the task of the pastor alone but the whole church. That, of course, is exactly what the Final Report says.

If the ecumenical family is, as Protestant theology says it is, a "little" church, and if it is, as the Second Vatican Council says it is, a domestic church, then it is necessarily a servant church. The spouses are called to serve one another and their nuclear family. They are called also to serve their churches and, as the Puritan ethic is wont to say, the various other commonwealths in which they live. In this service, the Second Vatican Council teaches, "The Christian family, which springs from marriage as a reflection of the loving covenant uniting Christ with the church and is a participation in that covenant, will manifest to all people the Savior's living presence in the world and the genuine nature of the church. This the family will do by the mutual love of the spouses, by their generous fruitfulness, their solidarity and faithfulness, and by the loving way in which all the members of the family work together."[4]

One very specific service that ecumenical couples, especially successful ecumenical couples, can and ought to offer to their churches is the pastoral care of other ecumenical marriages. It is clear today that care is best delivered, not by a pastor alone, but in a peer-to-peer model by ecumenical couples who have gained both useful insights from their own lived experience of ecumenical marriage and the Christian freedom and courage to live according to their insights.

A domestic ecumenical church that is manifestly a servant church constitutes a powerful gift and challenge to the larger churches and to the world they are called to serve. When Christian churches are divided from one another, and when the world is even more seriously divided, an ecumenical servant family provides a vital and vibrant sign that people who differ about important things can still live and serve together in mutual love and peace and helpfulness. Such a Christian family is truly a light to the nations, a *lumen gentium.*

Though pastoral care is the responsibility of the whole church and never of pastors alone, pastors still have an important and distinct pastoral responsibility. It is their task to preach the Gospel unceasingly to their congregations, to lead them to an ever more concrete understanding of the Gospel, and to empower them to enter into an ever-fuller practice of their servant mission. Pastors are to fulfill this task with all the means available to them—their preaching, their manifold teaching outside of liturgical gatherings, and in the countless service groups which they organize in their parishes.

The best pre-marital and post-marital care pastors can provide for Christian marriages of all kinds is drawing their parishioners into a worshipping, learning, serving church, "where they may know themselves to be a part of the ongoing People of God who have been called to live together under the Lordship of Jesus Christ and to minister to the needs of the world."[5] Because of traditionally negative (and stubborn) ecclesiastical attitudes toward ecumenical marriages, that care is even more necessary for ecumenical marriages than for same-faith marriages.

Ecumenical Education

If the pastor and the church are to carry out their task of pastoral care for ecumenical marriages, both must be educated ecumenically. That means that both will have to understand, not only the theology and laws of their own tradition concerning marriage, but also those of other Christian traditions. Spouses who seek to enter into an ecumenical marriage must understand each of their traditions as fully as possible, so that they can come to understand and appreciate one another more fully, and so they can educate their children ecumenically. For this to happen, they must prepare themselves ecumenically, not just in the few weeks that precede their wedding, but throughout their entire marriage.

Christians often are not only *ill*-informed about one another's doctrinal positions, but are also downright *mis*informed. Protestants, as we have noted several times, frequently accuse the Catholic church, for instance, of a sacramental doctrine that makes grace automatic. Though such is not, and never has been, the official teaching of the Catholic church, the polemical context of the Reformation gave rise to this distortion and propagated it as official teaching. The fact that most Roman Catholics, including some Catholic preachers, do not grasp their church's official teaching, with its complementary balance between the sacramental action and the living faith of a recipient, does nothing to help the situation.

The reality of Roman Catholic doctrine is that a sacrament is an efficient symbol of grace only when the desire of God to grace a man or a woman (*opus operatum*) is matched by the desire of the man or woman to be graced (*opus operantis*). Only when the two coincide, only when the encounter between God and humans is dialogical, does the sacrament become a fruitful sign of grace.

Catholics, similarly, frequently accuse the Protestant traditions of reducing Christian marriage to nothing more than a natural, social institution. Though such is not, and never has been, the teaching of any Protestant confession, again the polemics of the Reformation distorted the true reformed doctrine of marriage as covenant, and propagated the distortion as official Protestant teaching. Again, that most Protestants, including some pastors, do not grasp their church's careful teaching on marriage as covenant does nothing to help the situation. The reality of Protestant teaching, as I have sought to show, is that Christian marriage is a covenant rooted in the covenants of God with God's people and of Christ with Christ's church, and that the family deriving from such covenant is a chosen people, a fellowship of shared faith, a community of love and of service.

Only when Protestant and Catholic pastors and congregations have come to understand, and then to respect, each other's teaching will they be able to offer to both prospective and actual ecumenical spouses the marital preparation needed for a successful ecumenical marriage. The faith of parents, specifically the depth of their faith, is always a critical factor in the religious education of their children. It is an even more critical factor in the education of children of ecumenical marriages.

As the family is the first and, perhaps, the most vital cell of society, so the Christian family is the first and most vital cell of the church. It is, as I have repeatedly said, the domestic church, the image and representation of the universal church of Christ. It is in that domestic church that children will learn to value or not to value the Christ, the Gospel, and the church. If for no other reason than for the honest Christian education of their children, ecumenical parents must strive to understand and appreciate each other's faith as fully as possible. That way their children can consult both of them on both faiths, without having to resort to the divisive strategy, mentioned earlier, of consulting their father for one and their mother for the other. Such an approach will also ensure that nothing explicitly or implicitly derogatory about the other's faith will ever be said around the children.

Ecumenical In-Laws There is another important group of people to be considered here: the parents of the prospective ecumenical bride and groom. Parents may have concerns about the differences between the churches and, therefore, between their son or daughter and the one he or she is planning to marry. They may fear the loss of faith either through conversion or indifference. They may worry where the wedding will take place, which church the ecumenical couple will attend, and what faith their grandchildren will be reared in. They may never have heard of ecumenism and may cause great irritation or anger after the wedding by trying to convert the spouse not of their tradition.

An honest conversation with both sets of parents may dispel the tensions. They can be told of contemporary ecumenism and of the changes in the attitudes of the churches toward one another. They can be told how important their different faiths are to the prospective spouses, and how each respects the faith of the other. They can be told that their children have discussed the things that are bothering them, that they have made jointly-acceptable decisions about them, and that they are now asking their parents to respect their decisions, even though they would have preferred different ones. If need be, they can be asked to talk to their minister or priest about the marriage and what it entails. Once they realize that the potential points of conflict have been worked out, parents may be less distressed about an ecumenical marriage for their children.

The Promise of Children

My friend Gail once confided in me that "children present the real problem in an ecumenical marriage." As a parent, I easily recognized the truth of that statement, for children present the real challenge in any marriage. How are they to be reared and nurtured? How are they to be disciplined?

How are they to be educated? In an ecumenical marriage, those questions focus specifically on how children are to be nurtured and educated religiously.

A frequent problem is that such questions often emerge quite late in a couple's life together. They emerge, for instance, when the time comes for the baptism of the first child, a time often fraught with emotion which interferes with open and frank discussion. Parents need to realize that the religious upbringing of a child is dependent on more than baptism. It is dependent also, and more crucially, on religious modeling by the parents. The decision about what modeling will be offered clearly ought to be made before marriage. That decision necessarily includes a decision about the baptism of the children.

In order to obtain a dispensation to marry non-Catholic Christians, Catholic partners are required to promise to do all in their power to rear the children of their marriages as Catholics. This promise about children has led and continues to lead to much misunderstanding and resentment on the part of both partners. When balanced against related teachings of the Catholic church, however, it appears quite unnecessary. It is a requirement that ought to be dropped.

The promise concerning children potentially touches three parties: Catholic partners, non-Catholic partners, and children resulting from their love. For Catholic partners, the promise is no more than an assurance that they understand their obligations as Catholics. It adds no new obligation in conscience, but only makes explicit an obligation already existing by the simple fact that they are Catholics. As Catholics, they are *ipso facto* obliged to rear their children as Catholics. Consciousness raising concerning the religious training of children is certainly a good thing, but it could be achieved as easily, and with less damage to ecumenical relations, by a simple reminder to Catholic partners of their already existing obligation.

In pre-ecumenical days, non-Catholic partners were obliged to promise to provide for the Catholic baptism and education of their children. In 1970, Pope Paul VI's Apostolic Letter, *Matrimonia Mixta*, freed them from any obligation to promise anything. For them, the promise Catholic partners are required to make is simply informational, a clarification of the state of mind and of the desires of the Catholic partners. Again, this information could be generated in ways more human and less hurtful than a required promise.

Religious Education: A Mutual Decision   In its Declaration on Religious Freedom, the Second Vatican Council taught explicitly that "parents have the right to determine, in accordance with their own religious beliefs, the kind of religious education that their children are to receive."[6] In agreement with all other churches, the Catholic church recognizes today that the education of their children is the right and the obligation of *both* parents together and is not, therefore, to be assigned in advance to one parent over the other. The promise required of a Catholic partner specifies only that he or she will "do all in my power" to ensure that the children of the marriages are raised as Catholics. It does not guarantee that the children *will in fact* be raised Catholics. All decisions about the children, including the decision about their religious upbringing, are joint and free decisions of both parents, never of the Catholic spouse alone.

The Catholic spouse alone does not have unlimited power. The phrase, "do all in my power," is therefore to be understood as placing the free unity of the spouses before any obligation of the Catholic partner. It is to be understood as affirming the non-Catholic spouse's equal partnership in the ecumenical marriage, respecting that spouse's religious conviction and conscience, and promising to do all in one's power to reach a decision about the upbringing of the children with which both spouses are comfortable.

This interpretation was affirmed by Pope Paul VI in his *Matrimonia Mixta*. After having stated that the Catholic partner in a mixed marriage is obliged *"as far as possible* to see to it that the children are baptized and brought up" in the Catholic faith, he immediately adds that the question of the children's faith is not the Catholic partner's alone. "The problem of the children's education is a particularly difficult one, in view of the fact that *both husband and wife are bound by that responsibility and may by no means ignore it or any of the obligations connected with it."*[7]

John Paul II reiterates both the difficulty and the church's unchanging attitude toward it. He cites Paul VI on the obligation of the Catholic spouse with respect to the children, and immediately adds a caution: "There must be borne in mind the particular difficulties inherent in the relationships between husband and wife with regard to respect for religious freedom. This freedom could be violated either by undue pressure to make the partner change his or her beliefs or by placing obstacles in the way of the free manifestation of these beliefs by religious practice."[8]

No promise should ever be allowed to be an empty one. But the promise Catholics are required to make before marrying a non-Catholic clashes so significantly with the firm conviction of the churches (and the free faith of the partners) that the upbringing of the children is the mutual right and responsibility of *both* parents that it is an almost-empty promise. It would be best for everyone if it were dropped.

The third group the promise about children touches, the children, is frequently forgotten. Their churches and their parents become so engrossed in staking out their various obligations and inviolable rights that they give little thought to the rights of the children. But children, too, have inviolable rights which need to be taken into account.

The same Decree on Religious Freedom, which safeguards the rights of parents in the education of their children, safeguards also the rights of children in their relationship with their God. It teaches, for instance, that "man's [read *a child's]* response to God in faith must be free. Therefore, no one [read *no child*] is to be forced to embrace the Christian faith against his will."[9] It states again that "the doctrine of the church that no one [read *no child]* is to be coerced into faith has always stood firm."[10] The Decree on the Church's Missionary Activity makes the same point: "The church strictly forbids forcing anyone [read *any child*] to embrace the faith, or alluring or enticing people [read *children*] by unworthy techniques."[11]

The position that faith is, and therefore always must be, free, has been the unbroken Catholic tradition for centuries. It was even enshrined as the law of the Catholic church in 1917: "No one is to be forced to embrace the Catholic faith against his will" (Can. 1351). All that remains is for churches and for parents, ecumenical and Catholic alike, to start taking it seriously in the case of their own children.

Much of the trauma associated with mixed marriages in earlier generations no longer happens. It is, nevertheless, foolish to expect the limitations of the traditional approach to mixed marriage will be overcome easily. That will not happen, I suggest, until there are two practical realizations. There must be, first, a realization that ecumenical marriages are not problems for churches and for spouses but gifts of grace and challenges for continued growth. There must be, secondly, a realization that joint pastoral training of pastors is needed to prepare people specifically for fully understood ecumenical marriages.

A Call for Cooperative Preparation   I know all of the churches already have in place norms and procedures for preparing partners for ecumenical marriages. They are norms and procedures, however, as I have suggested, which have been developed in isolation from, and often in direct confrontation with, one another. Only when there are programs of joint preparation, both of pastors and of ecumenical spouses, prospective and actual, only when Lutherans explain Lutheranism and Catholics explain Catholicism, will there be genuine hope of overcoming the traditional distortions and confrontations which keep Christians apart.

There is an ancient East African proverb that Christians might heed here: "The life of the Kraal is understood by the one who sleeps there, not by the one who pays a visit there in the morning."[12] Only when the preparation for ecumenical marriage is done by those who sleep "in the Kraal" will the churches have provided proof that they are ready and willing to respond pastorally to the challenges presented by ecumenical marriages.

The Canonical Form

The Roman Catholic church requires that, for an ecumenical marriage to be recognized as valid, a Catholic spouse must celebrate it according to the form established in Canon Law. That canonical form is enunciated in Canon 1108: "Only those marriages are valid which are contracted in the presence of the local ordinary or parish priest or of the priest or deacon delegated by either of them, who, in the presence of two witnesses, assists." Though it is usually possible today to arrange a wedding ceremony in which a Protestant pastor can take part, the restriction of form is still quite unnecessary. It was introduced originally by the Council of Trent, not for some compelling-for-all-time theological reason, but as a practical measure to counteract the medieval scourge of the clandestine or secret marriage.

The Catholic canonical and theological doctrine is that the persons named in Canon 1108 are required to be present only as witnesses to the giving of consent. Catholic doctrine, which teaches that the couple administers the sacrament of marriage to one another, differs from Orthodox doctrine, which teaches that a priest is the minister. The priest merely *assists* at the Roman Catholic ceremony as a witness. Because of this, the *Code of Canon Law* lists cases in which the form prescribed by Canon 1108 need not be followed. It is time, I suggest, for one more exception in the case of ecumenical marriage.

There is no good reason, either theological or canonical or social, why an ecumenical marriage, in which a non-Catholic pastor witnesses the mutual giving and receiving of consent, should not be recognized as valid by the Catholic church. Canon 1127, 2 provides authority to permit just that in the case in which there are grave difficulties in the way of observing the canonical form. The National Conference of Catholic Bishops since January 1, 1971, has approved dispensations from the canonical form for a wide variety of such grave difficulties: "To achieve family harmony or to avoid family alienation, to obtain parental agreement to the marriage, to recognize the significant claims of relationship or special friendship with a non-Catholic minister, to permit the marriage in a church that has particular importance to the non-Catholic."[13]

Ease of dispensation, however, is not the question here, nor should it ever be. The present Catholic canonical form, was introduced solely to counter clandestine marriages by making publicly witnessed consent necessary for the validity of a marriage between Christians. It was not introduced for some eternally valid, theological reason. If the church could establish such a law in the sixteenth century to guarantee public consent and validity, it can just as easily establish in the twentieth century an alternative form requiring the assistance at an ecumenical marriage of either a Catholic or a Protestant pastor or both.

To object that a Protestant pastor cannot celebrate the nuptial mass apparently so integral to a Catholic wedding misses several points. However apt the celebration of the Lord's Supper might be to the Christian celebration of one-bodiness, and I shall take up this point in the next section, it is not essential to the celebration of the sacrament of marriage. Canon law is still adamant: "A marriage is brought into being by the lawfully manifested consent of persons who are legally capable" (Can. 1057, 1). "Lawfully manifested consent" still requires the presence of "the local ordinary or parish priest or of the priest or deacon delegated by either of them" (Can. 1108, 1), but it does not require the celebration of Mass.

So far, indeed, is the celebration of Mass not essential to the sacrament of marriage that, in the present ecumenical context, its celebration is actively discouraged in the case of ecumenical marriages. In their recent pastoral handbook for marriage preparation, the U.S. bishops recommend that, "given the restrictions on general invitations to eucharistic sharing, it is often a wise policy for an interreligious couple not to celebrate their wedding in the context of a nuptial mass." Their reason is instructive, and will lead us into our next section. The celebration of Mass, with the prohibition of intercommunion, "could serve to stress the split that exists between their own and their families' religious beliefs and practices rather than highlight the harmony of their love."[14]

What is required for a valid Christian marriage is, among other things, lawfully manifested consent. The official assistance at an ecumenical marriage of a Lutheran or a Reformed or an Episcopalian pastor would guarantee that consent every bit as much as the assistance of a Catholic priest or deacon. Such a minor change of form would dispense with the need for aggravating dispensations and would remove one of the quite unnecessary sources of pain and resentment in an ecumenical marriage. It would also, from the beginning, place the marriage and the spouses and the churches which bless them in the proper spirit of ecumenical cooperation.

Intercommunion

As we have just seen, the U.S. bishops advise that it is wise not to celebrate an ecumenical wedding in the context of a Mass, "given the restrictions on general invitations to eucharistic sharing" or intercommunion. This question of intercommunion is a vexed one in the churches. Though the Episcopal church has a policy of open communion with other believing Christians, all the other churches place restrictions on intercommunion. Because of their theology of ordination and of the power of orders which it confers, Catholics worry about the validity of non-Catholic orders and, therefore, of non-Catholic eucharists; Lutherans worry about agreement in the Gospel.[15] All consider communion to be the sign of full unity in the church; it should not, therefore, be offered to anyone not in full unity. Because it is usually on that argument that the present practice hinges, we need to consider it carefully.

The modern discussion in the Roman Catholic church begins, as it always begins these days, with the teaching of the Second Vatican Council: "As for common worship, it may not be regarded as a means to be used *indiscriminately* for the restoration of unity among Christians. Such worship depends chiefly on two principles: it should signify the unity of the church; it should provide a sharing in the means of grace. The fact that it should signify unity generally rules out common worship. *Yet the gaining of a needed grace sometimes commends it.*"[16] That statement was further specified in 1972 in an Instruction from the Secretariat for Promoting Christian Unity, which taught that baptized non-Catholics may be admitted to communion only for *true spiritual need.*[17] There are two key phrases in these statements. The first is that intercommunion may not be used *indiscriminately* as a means for promoting Christian unity. In this statement the Council acknowledges two things: first, the constant Catholic tradition that, as sacrament, the eucharist is not only a sign of, but also a means for promoting, unity among Christians; secondly, that eucharist therefore can and must be used discriminately as an effective means for the restoration of that unity. I suggest here only that, in the case of ecumenical spouses who fulfill the conditions I will enunciate in a moment, the discriminate use of intercommunion is a most effective sign of and means to the Christian unity between them.

To be fully discriminate, that is, as the dictionary says, to make full and clear distinctions, and to present no serious risk of indifference or scandal to the churches, the shared communion of ecumenical spouses must be regulated by certain conditions. The following seems to me a complete enumeration. First, the Christian spouse requesting the hospitality of communion must profess a firm belief in the presence of the Lord in eucharist, which is not the same thing as professing belief in any specific theological explanation of the mode of that presence. Secondly, she or he must request it freely, in good conscience, without pressure from the other spouse. Thirdly, she or he must be a regular communicant in her or his own church. Finally, there must be no danger of indifference or scandal, a situation which is easily avoided by a few words of explanation from the presider of the eucharistic celebration.

The second key phrase in the Roman documents is *true spiritual need.* I wish to raise the question whether in the case of spouses in true ecumenical marriages as I have defined them, spouses like Bill and Gail, who each believe in the presence of their common Lord at the Lord's table, such serious spiritual need is present. I suggest that it is.

As has been argued, spouses in an ecumenical marriage constitute a domestic church. As fully committed and active members of that church, they have achieved a twofold unity, a unity in one Christ that derives from their baptismal covenant (cf. Gal. 3:27–28) and a unity in one body deriving from their marital covenant (Gen. 2:24). Their double unity, which has been doubly blessed by both their churches, is a dynamic sacramental image of the unity between Christ and the church. That sacramental image of unity should not have to suffer division at eucharist simply because the Christian churches are slower than are Christian spouses at achieving unity. James Mackey's judgment here is correct. That "the Christian eucharist should be used to drive a wedge into the very symbol of Christ's union with the church represents an inexcusable assault upon the family, but that is because it represents an even more serious misunderstanding of the nature of Christianity itself."[18]

Paradoxically, the divided churches today constitute a problem for united ecumenical families more than such families constitute a problem for the churches. Precisely because they have become united in Christ, ecumenical families have a right to the eucharist which John Paul II correctly teaches "is the very source of Christian marriage." In the eucharist, "Christian spouses encounter the source from which their own marriage covenant flows, is interiorly structured and continuously renewed."[19] Spouses whose one-bodiness has been doubly blessed by the baptismal and matrimonial prayers of their churches ought not to be treated as two separate bodies at the eucharistic prayers of those same churches. They ought not to be denied access to such a crucial source of ongoing Christian and spousal unity.

Eucharistic Reconciliation The ecumenical reconciliation and unity lovingly and patiently built up in an ecumenical family has the serious need, and therefore the right, to be celebrated and strengthened by mutual eucharistic reconciliation and unity with both churches. What a witness to ecumenical reconciliation and unity that would be for the divided churches! Or, again to play on the Greek *marturion*, what a wonderfully saving martyrdom for the churches. Shared sacramental communion between believing and deeply unified spouses would be not only a ritual sign of their reconciled "one-bodiness" in Christ but also an instrument for the reconciled "one-bodiness" of their churches. It would be, that is, in the classical Roman Catholic theological language, a compelling sacrament of the reconciliation and unity to which all the Christian churches are summoned. It would hasten the day when the churches could move beyond debating questions of *inter*communion to celebrate together unrestricted *communion*.

To argue that, because eucharist is a sign of unity, only those who are in full unity with any given church should fully share in it, is to miss the theological fact that, as sacrament, it is not only a sign of unity already achieved but also an instrument of unity yet to be achieved. That unity is a grace sorely needed and ardently desired by many Christian believers, unmarried and married alike, and common celebration of eucharist and communion is a vehicle for such grace. That grace, in the specific case of the ecumenical marriages, and in the words of Vatican II cited above, commends intercommunion at least on occasion.

The churches are agreed that Jesus is the life-giving spirit (1 Cor. 15:45) who reconciles the estranged and breathes unity into his body, the church. They are further agreed that this life-giving, reconciling and uniting spirit is present most dynamically in eucharist. All that is required is the courage of these convictions, the courage to offer eucharistic hospitality to all Christians who confess the Lord's presence in eucharist, regardless of their ecclesiastical origin. It is to place the cart before the horse, yet once again, to hope for unity apart from eucharist and to offer eucharist only as a way to celebrate unity. In the case of ecumenical marriages, eucharistic communion is no more and no less than what it always has been, i.e., an eschatological sign of unity already achieved and a spirited means of unity still to be achieved.

As I mentioned in Chapter One, baptism is not a confessional matter. It not only introduces persons into this or that Christian confession, but also into the one church of Christ. Those who have been properly baptized, therefore, all share a Christian unity as brothers and sisters. That baptismal unity has led the German evangelical bishop, Hans Otto Wolber, to state with simple clarity that "Through baptism Christians are basically invited to the table of the Lord."[20]

When baptismal unity is extended and deepened in the marital communion of ecumenical spouses, the result is a communion in Christ so strikingly rare, even between the members of a given Christian confession, that its claim to shared communion at the table of the Lord ought never be questioned. Today, the religious facts on which Christians stand united far outweigh those on which they are divided. It is past the time when they should focus more on what positively unites them rather than on what negatively divides them.

School for Scandal?   I wish to make very clear what I am *not* suggesting and what I *am* suggesting. I am *not* suggesting that unconditioned and indiscriminate intercommunion be practiced, which would prove to be more a hindrance to than an instrument of genuine ecumenical unity. I am certainly *not* suggesting indiscriminate intercommunion at every ecumenical *wedding*. I *am* suggesting a very conditioned and discriminate intercommunion, one that is the result of very clear distinctions. And the major distinction and clarification is this: spouses must be truly ecumenical; they both must confess and rejoice in the presence of their common Lord in eucharist and seek marital "one-bodiness" with the Christian community in the Lord's Supper.

I *am* suggesting that, in the case of such ecumenical spouses, their spiritual need and desire to celebrate their Christian one-bodiness in the ritual of the Lord's one body is serious enough to meet the established Roman Catholic guidelines for intercommunion. I *am* further suggesting that the churches have a serious obligation to respond pastorally to this need by offering ecumenical spouses the Christian hospitality of shared communion. Finally, I *am* suggesting that, in the case of ecumenically married intercommunion, as in all Christian moral judgments, the judgment or *discrimen* is to be made by the spouses themselves who alone can know their intimate spiritual need. In the specific case of one-bodied ecumenical spouses, the theologies of their churches should not be allowed to obscure their unity under a common Creator, a common Christ, and a common Spirit.

The traditional response to this and similar suggestions is that a scandal will arise, which will be especially harmful for unspecified "little ones." I suggest that, when proper pastoral explanation is provided, such scandal has not and, therefore, will not, arise. It is an open secret that, in many dioceses throughout the world, married ecumenical couples are already sharing in communion in one another's churches, frequently with the knowing participation of their respective pastors.

In the cases in which I have first-hand knowledge, little scandal appears to have been either given or taken, perhaps because ecumenically-oriented pastors have taken seriously their pastoral responsibilities, and have sought to educate their congregations on the questions of discriminate, serious spiritual need. The simplest explanations given from the pulpit or in the classroom or in a bulletin quickly put scandal to rest. Scandal should never be confused with, or used as an excuse for, the pastoral failure of nerve to be expansively Christian.

Summary Questions for Discussion

1. Are you comfortable or uncomfortable with the claim that the pastoral care of ecumenical marriages (and of same-faith marriages too) is the task, not of the pastor alone, but of the whole church? What kind of model of church provides the basis for such a statement?

2. In your opinion, what kind of pastoral care do ecumenical marriages need most? Who, in your opinion, can best provide that care?

3. What is your evaluation of the claim that "parents have the right to determine, in accordance with their own religious beliefs, the kind of religious education their children are to receive"? What kind of religious education should that be in an ecumenical family?

4. In your opinion, is the canonical form presently required of all Roman Catholics necessary? If you think it is, explain why.

5. What do you think of intercommunion in general? In the specific case of ecumenical spouses?

Suggested Reading

Emminghaus, Joannes H. *The Eucharist: Essence, Form, Celebration* (Collegeville, Minnesota: Liturgical Press, 1978).

Fahey, Michael A. (ed.) *Catholic Perspectives on Baptism, Eucharist and Ministry* (Lanham, Maryland: University Press of America, 1986).

Faithful to Each Other Forever: A Catholic Handbook of Pastoral Help for Marriage Preparation (Washington, D.C.: United States Catholic Conference, 1989).

Hurley, Michael (ed.). *Beyond Tolerance* (London: Chapman, 1975).

Lynch, Thomas (ed.). *A Positive Vision for Family Life: A Resource Guide for Pope John Paul II's Apostolic Exhortation Familiaris Consortio* (Washington, D.C.: United States Catholic Conference, 1985).

Afterword

Christian marriage[1] is an intimate partnership of life and love, rooted in an irrevocable covenant of personal consent, in which a Christian man and a Christian woman mutually and totally bestow and accept each other. In an ecumenical marriage, the spouses' mutual bestowing and accepting embraces their different Christian faiths. Bill, a convinced-Catholic husband, accepts Gail, a convinced-Presbyterian wife, and she accepts him. Bill's complete acceptance of Gail embraces, necessarily, his acceptance of her *as* Presbyterian; Gail's total acceptance of Bill embraces, necessarily, her acceptance of him *as* Catholic.

Bill finds Gail, and therefore also her church, sufficiently catholic for him to be in total communion with her. Gail finds him, and therefore also his church, sufficiently reformed for her to be in total communion with him. To the degree that each accepts the other's Christian confession, they create a kind of a dual church membership. Both their churches ought to respect that dual membership, and grant it—and the Christian unity in baptism and covenantal marriage from which it springs—the right to be expressed and deepened in common communion with God.

Before the outcry becomes deafening, I want to add my voice to it. The dual membership I propose is an anomaly, as is the ecclesiastical prohibition that denies a united Christian husband and wife common communion at the one table of the Lord. Both, however, are minor anomalies compared to the major anomaly that spawns them, namely, the divisions among the Christian churches. I am suggesting only that, if the churches cannot yet deal with this major anomaly, they can at least sanction the minor ones. It may, after all, provide a creative step toward reconciling all the world's Christian churches.

Total unity within an ecumenical family, committed membership in two Christian churches, regularly shared communion expressing and deepening both: these are gifts and challenges ecumenical marriages bring to the present context of a divided Christian community. They are gifts to the degree that they manifest yet again the achievability of Paul's ancient insight: "There is neither Jew nor Greek, there is neither slave nor free, there is neither male nor female, for you are all one person in Christ Jesus" (Gal. 3:28). True ecumenical marriages are challenges for they urge churches to learn that there is neither Catholic nor Presbyterian, neither Anglican nor Lutheran, neither Baptist nor Orthodox. In the one church of God, there is only Christ who "is all and in all" (Col. 3:11). As Paul might say, to him be the glory for ever and ever (cf. Gal. 1:5).

NOTES

PREFACE

1. *Centerpiece* from the Newsletter of the Association of Interchurch Families. Available from the Old Bakery, Danehill, Sussex RH 17 7ET, England.

CHAPTER ONE

1. On the Family *(Familiaris Consortio,)* n. 78.

2. Dean Hoge and Kathleen M. Ferry, *Empirical Research on Interfaith Marriage in America* (Washington, D.C.: United States Catholic Conference, 1981), 1.

3. *Familiaris Consortio,* n. 69.

4. *Familiaris Consortio,* n. 78.

5. *Growth in Agreement: Reports and Agreed Statements of Ecumenical Conversations on a World Level,* ed. Harding Meyer and Lukas Vischer (Mahwah, New Jersey: Paulist Press, 1984), 62 and 128. (This work will be cited hereafter as *GA).*

6. *Acta Apostolicae Sedis,* 35 (1943): 199. Emphasis added. (This work will be cited hereafter as *AAS.)*

7. "Dogmatic Constitution on the Church," n. 8, in *The Documents of Vatican II,* ed. Walter M. Abbott (London: Chapman, 1967), 23. (This work will be cited hereafter as *DV.)*

8. "Decree on Ecumenism," n. 3, in *DV* 345.

9. *GA* 284.

10. Juan Alfaro, "Faith," in *Sacramentum Mundi: An Encyclopedia of Theology* (New York: Herder, 1968), II:315.

11. Denzinger–Schonmetzer, *Enchiridion Symbolorum,* n. 1532. (Cited hereafter as *DS.)* Cf. *DS* 1529.

12. *DS* 1606.

13. *DS* 1310.

14. "Constitution on the Sacred Liturgy," n. 59. *DV* 158.

15. *Summa Theologiae,* III, 59, 3 ad 1.

16. See Wilson Yates, "The Protestant View of Marriage," in *Journal of Ecumenical Studies* 22 (1985): pp. 41–42; also "Pastoral Constitution on the Church in the Modern World," n. 48, *DV* 250–252.

17. "Pastoral Constitution on the Church," n. 11, *DV* 29.

18. James P. Mackey, *Modern Theology: A Sense of Direction* (New York: Oxford University Press, 1987), p. 153.

CHAPTER TWO

1. "Pastoral Constitution on the Church," n. 48, *DV* 250.

2. Paul Palmer, "Christian Marriage: Contract or Covenant," in *Theological Studies*, 33 (1972), p. 639.

3. "Pastoral Constitution on the Church," n. 25, *DV* 225.

4. Ibid., n. 48, *DV* 250.

5. Ibid., n. 50, *DV* 253–255.

6. For an extended treatment of this notion of symbol, see Michael G. Lawler, *Symbol and Sacrament: A Contemporary Sacramental Theology* (Mahwah, New Jersey: Paulist Press, 1987).

7. "Pastoral Constitution on the Church," n. 11, *DV* 29.

8. Karl Rahner, "History of the World and Salvation History," in *Theological Investigations*, Vol. 5 (London: Darton, Longman, Todd, 1966), p. 98.

9. This section is inspired by Wilson Yates, "The Protestant View of Marriage," pp. 41–54.

10. "Social Principles of the United Methodist Church," *The Discipline* (Nashville: The United Methodist Publishing House, 1984).

11. *Ephesians. The Anchor Bible* (New York: Doubleday, 1974) ,p. 618.

12. *The Worshipbook Services* (Philadelphia: Westminster Press, 1970), p. 67.

13. *The Rites* (New York: Pueblo Publishing Company, 1976), p. 544.

CHAPTER THREE

1. See J.J. von Allmen, "Ordination—A Sacrament? A Protestant Reply," *Concilium*, Vol. 4, No. 8 (1972), p. 40.

2. See Lawler, *Symbol and Sacrament*, pp. 29–34.

3. *Code of Canon Law* (1983), Can. 1057, 2.

4. See John Giles Milhaven, "Conjugal Sexual Love and Contemporary Moral Theology," in *Theological Studies* 35 (1974), pp. 704–705.

5. *Summa Theologiae*, III (Supple.), 65, 1, corp.

6. For more detail, see Michael G. Lawler, *Secular Marriage, Christian Sacrament* (Mystic, Connecticut: Twenty-Third Publications, 1985), pp. 23–37.

7. Milhaven, "Conjugal Sexual Love," n. 15, 700.

8. *Ibid.,* 705.

9. The thoughts in this section on *eros* and *agape* were stimulated by Helmut Gollwitzer, *Song of Love: A Biblical Understanding of Sex* (Philadelphia: Fortress Press, 1979).

CHAPTER FOUR

1. Cf. *Mishna,* Git. IX, 10

2. Those who wish to survey the opinions may consult: A. Myre, "Dix ans d'exegese sur le divorce dans le Nouveau Testament," *Le Divorce: l'Eglise catholique ne devrait-elle pas modifier son attitude seculaire a l'egard de l'indissolubilite de mariage* (Montreal: Dies, 1973); J. Fitzmyer, "The Matthean Divorce Texts and Some New Palestinian Evidence," *Theological Studies,* 37 (1976), pp. 197–226; Bruce J. Malina, "Does Porneia Mean Fornication?" *Novum Testamentum* XIV (1972): pp. 10–17; E. Haenchen, *The Acts of the Apostles: A Commentary* (Philadelphia: Westminster, 1971); and Corrado Marucci, *Parole di Gesu sul divorzio* (Naples: Morcelliana, 1982).

3. Bruce J. Malina, *The New Testament World: Insights from Cultural Anthropology* (Atlanta: John Knox Press, 1981), pp. 118–21.

4. Theodore Mackin, *Divorce and Remarriage* (Mahwah, New Jersey: Paulist Press, 1984), p. 86.

5. Kevin T. Kelly, *Divorce and Second Marriage: Facing the Challenge* (New York: Seabury Press, 1983), p. 39.

6. *AAS* 33 (1941): 425–426.

7. *GA,* 288–289.

8. *AAS* 44 (1952), p. 271.

9. See "Propositions on the Doctrine of Christian Marriage," in *Origins,* Sept. 28, 1978, p. 237.

10. Constitution on the Sacred Liturgy, n. 59, *DV* 158.

11. For a fuller development of the point sketched here, see Lawler, *Symbol and Sacrament,* pp. 36–45.

12. Anyone desiring a fuller treatment might wish to consult Michael G. Lawler, *Secular Marriage, Christian Sacrament* (Mystic, Connecticut: Twenty-Third Publications, 1985); Jack Dominian, *Christian Marriage* (London: Darton, Longman, and Todd, 1968); Walter Kasper, *Theology of Christian Marriage* (New York: Crossroad, 1981); Theodore Mackin, *What is Marriage?* (Mahwah, New Jersey: Paulist Press,

1982); Elizabeth M. Tetlow and Louis M. Tetlow, *Partners in Service: Towards a Biblical Theology of Christian Marriage* (Lanham, Maryland.: University Press of America, 1983); and David M. Thomas, *Christian Marriage: A Journey Together* (Wilmington: Michael Glazier, 1983).

CHAPTER FIVE

1. *GA*, 292.

2. "Pastoral Constitution on the Church," n. 1, *DV* 15; cf. *ibid.* n. 9, *DV* 26; *ibid.* n. 48, *DV* 79; "Constitution on the Sacred Liturgy," n. 5, *DV* 140 and n. 26, *DV* 147; Decree on the Missionary Activity of the Church, n. 5, *DV* 589.

3. See Lawler, *Symbol and Sacrament*, p. 216.

4. "The Church in the Modern World," n. 48, *DV* 252.

5. *GA*, 292.

6. N. 5, *DV* 683.

7. *AAS* 62 (1970), 259.

8. *Familiaris Consortio*, n. 78.

9. N. 10, *DV*, 689.

10. N. 12, *ibid.*, 692–693

11. N. 13, *ibid*, 600.

12. Cited in V. Neckebrouck, "Literary Arguments on African Polygamy," *Theology Digest*, 35 (1988), p. 122.

13. Cited in *Doing the Truth in Charity*, ed. Thomas F. Stransky and John B. Sheerin (Mahwah, New Jersey: Paulist Press, 1982), p. 146.

14. *Faithful to Each Other Forever*, Section 3.

15. See George A. Lindbeck, "A Lutheran View of Intercommunion with Roman Catholics," and Avery Dulles, "Intercommunion Between Lutherans and Roman Catholics," *Journal of Ecumenical Studies*, 13 (1976), pp. 242–249, 250–257.

16. Decree on Ecumenism, n. 8, *DV* 352. Emphasis added.

17. "De Peculiaribus Casibus Admittendi Alios Christianos ad Communionem Eucharisticam in Ecclesia Catholica," *AAS* 64 (1972): 518–525. Emphasis added.

18. James P. Mackey, *Modern Theology*, p. 153.

19. *Familiaris Consortio*, n. 57.

20. Cited in Kenan B. Osborne, "Contemporary Understanding of the Eucharist: A Survey of Catholic Thinking," *Journal of Ecumenical Studies*, 13 (1976), p. 193.

AFTERWORD

1. While the ideas expressed in this Afterword are entirely my own, they have been influenced by Geoffrey Wainwright's essay, "The Ecclesiological Significance of Interchurch Marriage," in *Beyond Tolerance*, ed. Michael Hurley (London: Chapman, 1975), pp. 104–109. I am happy to acknowledge here my debt to Professor Wainwright.